PRESENTING
FOR HUMANS

ADVANCE PRAISE FOR
PRESENTING FOR HUMANS

"Lisa Braithwaite is willing to talk about the real and raw aspects of public speaking, to offer advice that encourages speakers to reflect upon their craft and rise to meet their potential. Her voice is imperative for anyone who stands in front of others with a message to be heard."

— Ellen Bremen —
Professor, Communication Studies

"Full of practical tips, illustrated by interesting examples. Use it as a reference when the need arises, or read it from cover to cover. Either way, your presentations will be more engaging and effective."

— Ron Adler —
Communication Textbook Author

"Where was this book when I started speaking over a decade ago?! All I can say is: better late than never. This thing is packed with tips and insights that will help any speaker take things to the next level."

— Jason Kotecki, CSP —
Artist, Author, and Professional Speaker
EscapeAdulthood.com

PRESENTING FOR HUMANS

INSIGHTS FOR SPEAKERS ON
DITCHING PERFECTION
AND
CREATING CONNECTION

LISA BRAITHWAITE

Red Letter Publishing, Austin

Presenting for Humans: Insights for Speakers on Ditching Perfection and Creating Connection
Copyright © 2017 by Lisa Braithwaite.
All rights reserved.

Book typeset by Kevin Williamson
Cover illustration by Paolo Fabbri

Created in the United States of America

23 22 21 20 19 18 17   1 2 3 4 5

ISBN 978-0-9981714-1-8 (paperback)

ACKNOWLEDGEMENTS

This book was inspired by friends, colleagues, business owners, store clerks, restaurant servers and other service providers, as well as government officials, business leaders, speakers, entertainers and athletes—most of whom I've never met. I appreciate all the "fodder" you've provided for my writing over the past ten years, and the lessons I've learned and insights gained from my interactions and experiences with you.

Huge thanks and gratitude to everyone who has encouraged me to finally get this book written, and to everyone who has asked, "When is your book coming out?" I have never had a single doubter in my life, a single person who didn't believe in me, except myself! Everyone who has ever kicked me in the butt, held me accountable, or reminded me that "done is better than perfect" is part of any success I achieve with this book, including the mere act of getting it published.

To name names, my accountability partners Tammy, Elizabeth and Amy have lent an ear to many outpourings of frustration, indecision and anxiety. My coach, Alicia Forest, gently but firmly nudges me in the direction of my future greatness. My OBBW sisters, Beth, Sandra, Debbie, Gail, Andrea, Brigitte, Natanya, Paula, Linda, Crystal and Clare (and more!) have been there over the years when I've needed a boost or advice.

Jean, Carolyn, Alice and Elaine gave constructive and comprehensive feedback on the first draft of the book that empowered me to trust my message, my direction, and my voice as I moved forward.

My book coach, Cathy Fyock, was the first book "Sherpa" who actually grasped—and got excited about—the idea of turning my blog into a book, forging ahead with a process we both uncovered together.

My husband Rudy has this steadfast belief and certainty that I have endless potential and can achieve anything I set my mind to. I can't imagine where I would be in my business without his confidence in my abilities, considering that his confidence in me frequently outweighs my confidence in myself.

DEDICATION

This book is dedicated to everyone who has ever read and commented on a blog post or has emailed me with a reply to an article I've published in my newsletter. Sometimes writers wonder if anyone is reading. You've given me a reason to keep writing, to keep teaching, and to keep growing as a speaker and a coach.

HOW TO GET YOUR FREE DOWNLOADS

1. Visit www.coachlisab.com/pfh-form.html to register.

2. Enter your name and email address into the form.

3. Look for a confirmation email – you'll be asked to click the link to confirm your registration.

4. You'll receive a link by email to access your downloads. That email will contain a password.

5. Follow the link. Download. Enjoy!

CONTENTS

INTRODUCTION

In 2005, I started my public speaking coaching business. It was out of necessity, really; I had been laid off from three nonprofit jobs in four years, and I was getting a little peeved about not having control of my own destiny (and paycheck).

Within a year, I was blogging, because in 2006, there was no Facebook, no Twitter, only blogs and forums. And if you had a message to share and you wanted to engage with a wide – even international – audience, blogs were the way to go.

One of my earliest blog posts referenced Steve Eggleston, AKA The Eggman, with this quote:

"I stopped worrying about what people would think about me when I realized how seldom people think about anyone but themselves."

There it is, in a nutshell. It's the concept behind everything I teach, although I'm not sure I could have said it so eloquently.

Your audience isn't thinking about you; they're thinking about themselves – whatever that means at any given time.

They're thinking, "I hope this presentation isn't a drag, because I have a ton of work to do." They're thinking, "I hope there's a gluten-free option for lunch, because I forgot to list my dietary preferences." They're thinking, "I hope there's a break soon, because I really need to pee." They're thinking, "What am I missing on Facebook?"

And yes, sometimes they're even thinking, "I hope I learn something really mind-blowing from this presentation that will change the way I think, the way I live, or the way I work."

As speakers, whether advanced or inexperienced, whether speaking in ballrooms or in board meetings, we all face the same challenges.

How do we create compelling, relevant, and useful content for our audiences in a way that they are able to take our messages and use them to transform their work or lives?

How do we engage our audiences and make a human connection, so that they can envision for themselves the possibilities we present and take steps to achieve them?

And what kind of growth and personal development do we have to embrace to get ourselves into the right mindset with the right attitude to support and encourage our audience's growth?

It's not as hard as you think to make these shifts and transformations, both for your own benefit and for that of your audience. In fact, it's as easy as having lunch at your neighborhood deli.

If you've ever had a stimulating conversation with a fellow customer in line at the grocery store, you know what I'm talking about. Looking at our everyday experiences and encounters with fresh eyes gives us new perspectives on all aspects of our lives, including speaking.

For me, being open to learning - wherever and whenever it chooses to find me - has allowed me to stretch and expand what I used to think about speaking.

There was a time when I thought the most important things about speaking were artfully using my hands, or impressing people with big words, or heroically avoiding saying "um." (I will confess here that I was on the speech team in high school, and perhaps some of the habits I learned there needed to be unlearned.) Yes, I thought speaking was all about **me**.

But presenting is so much more than just standing in front of a group of people and pontificating. It's so much more than "telling," or "lecturing" or "conveying information."

Unfortunately, most of us spend our time in rooms where the presentations have no energy, no life, no engagement, no love, and no soul. We could easily replace the human on stage with a robot, and who would know the difference?

We sit through presentations that are irrelevant, boring, and tedious, and sometimes we feel like the life is being sucked right out of us. As a friend described to me once, pointless presentations don't just waste our time, they **steal** our time. I don't want to spend one more minute listening to a presentation that is going to steal time that I will never get back again, and I don't want to inflict such presentations on other people!

We are humans, speaking to humans, and we neglect to take the full scope of this into account. We are thinking beings, yes. But we are also feeling beings. We are imperfect beings. We are impulsive and annoying and funny and rude and thoughtful beings. And we are infinitely creative beings.

I want to help you view speaking in a new way, through my eyes and through my everyday experiences, so that you can go apply **your** life experiences to your speaking and bring your own unique perspective to your audiences. And whether you're trying to master this skill so you can make a living at it or just trying to get through those team updates your boss keeps asking you to do, you will find new perspective here.

The book is divided into themed chapters: Preparation, Confidence, Fun, Connection, Service, Experience, Standing Out, and Mindset. These are the core themes that I teach and coach on, and the public speaking concepts that I find to be most critical to a speaker's success.

Feel free to jump around and find the chapters that are most relevant to your needs in the moment. Each section within the chapter was written to stand alone, and also further fleshes out the main theme of the chapter.

This book also poses self-reflection questions for you to consider. No one can answer these questions for you, because only you know what your goals and intentions are for being a better speaker. But I hope these questions will help guide you to finding your own objectives for speaking, your own intentions for your audiences, and your own desired results for the personal and professional development goals that you can achieve through speaking.

You'll find downloadable worksheets and checklists at www.coachlisab.com/pfh-form.html that you can use to answer the questions and make additional practice notes. I've highlighted those tools throughout the book.

Enjoy this guide to how everyday encounters and experiences can make you a better speaker, a more joyful speaker, a more captivating speaker, a more effective speaker, and, most important, a more human speaker.

1 MAKE **PREPARATION** A PRIORITY

Ahhh, preparation. The bane of every speaker's existence.

I have a theory about why preparation is so painful and difficult for speakers. I think that speakers who "wing it" are far more afraid of failure and rejection than those who prepare, although it might seem to be the opposite.

See, if you wing it and succeed – your audience applauds, your jokes land, you come across as articulate and compelling, and people want to meet you afterward – then you can be relieved and pleasantly surprised. You can even tell yourself, "I'm good at winging it."

If you wing it and fail – your jokes bomb, you lose your focus, your ideas aren't organized, the audience is polite but bored – you can always tell yourself, "Well, I didn't really prepare. If I had prepared, it would have been **so much** better."

What happens if you prepare and you still fail? That's the ultimate reality you're trying to avoid, because perhaps then you've really wasted your time. You think, "What's the point? If I prepare, I still suck, so why bother?"

We tell ourselves so many stories about ourselves. And many of them are based on creating the hard armor of protection. We (try to) protect ourselves from looking foolish, from looking like we tried too hard, from looking like we might be human, with visible flaws. So we hold ourselves back, afraid to take too big a step or put ourselves too far out in front of the crowd. If no one notices us, we can't get hurt.

But what if you changed your whole mindset about speaking, or your whole mindset about the audience? What if you actually made a sincere effort and committed yourself to excellence, connection, engagement, and transformation?

What if, through "failing" (although there's no such thing in speaking or life – just "learning"), you were able to grow and expand and become a more compelling speaker than you ever imagined? What if you were able to touch your audiences and move them to action in ways that only seem like fantasy right now?

If you care about making a difference to your audiences and not just getting your presentations over with, you'll have to push yourself further than you ever have. It's not as easy as winging it, but it's going to be worth it.

In this section, look for lessons for speakers using examples from professional cyclists, event planners, and pie crust!

1. BUILD YOUR PUBLIC SPEAKING IMMUNITY

During cold and flu season, it's a challenge to stay healthy. Your immune system plays a big role in how many times you get sick each year. Did you know that, once you become infected with and fight off a particular strain of a virus, it won't ever make you sick again?

There are estimated to be 150-200 different cold viruses out there; you won't catch the same virus twice because once you've suffered through it, your body has built immunity to that particular strain.

When you get sick (or get a flu shot), your body actually gets stronger, protecting you against more and more viruses each year.

It's the same with public speaking!

The more often you speak, the more often you expose yourself to different venues, audiences, and circumstances, the stronger you become as a speaker.

You learn how to deal with any size group, any challenge, any unexpected questions, any unforeseen mishaps.

Unfortunately, unlike the common cold, you may experience the same setback twice.

For example, you may find that you face a hostile audience member once a year –or once a week, depending on your topic!

But increasing your public speaking exposure allows you to get better over time at how you handle confrontations. So eventually, the hostile audience member feels more like a sniffle than a full-blown cold.

The first few times you encounter challenges, you might want to crawl into bed with a cup of tea and an aspirin, but the more experience you get, the stronger you become.

The only way to build your public speaking immunity is to get out there and do it!

• •

SELF-REFLECTION
How are you building your public speaking immunity?

• •

2. WHAT CAN A SPEAKER LEARN FROM A TATTOO ARTIST?

Tattoo artists must be some of the most confident professionals around, along with firefighters and astronauts. Imagine how fearless you must be in your abilities to touch a needle to someone's skin and leave a permanent mark!

Here are a few things I've learned from watching tattoo artists.

A tattoo artist must merge the client's wishes with what the artist knows will actually be a good tattoo.

When I got my second tattoo, I brought a tiny Celtic border design with me. It was red with a black outline. The tattoo artist looked at it and said, "It's too small." He explained that, in this intricate design, the colors would bleed together over time if the lines were not spaced farther apart. He also suggested a color change, adding a yellow highlight to make the design look more 3-D.

He knew exactly what would look right and what would last, and even though I thought I knew what I wanted, he persuaded me that his idea was better. And he was right!

As a speaker, you're the expert. You've been invited to speak because you have knowledge, skills, or perspective that your audience can learn from. You must be persuasive and convincing in your arguments while also listening to and respecting the audience's point of view. It's not always easy, especially when speaking on controversial or difficult subject matter. But if you don't stick to your guns and stay resolute in your message, you will not succeed as a speaker.

A tattoo artist must continually keep practicing, learning, and growing in order to build skills and confidence.
Imagine a tattoo artist saying, "I'm scared to make a mistake, so I'm

going to avoid tattooing as much as possible." It's ridiculous, right? But inexperienced speakers frequently avoid speaking out of fear of the unknown.

A tattoo artist knows that the way to overcome weaknesses and build on strengths is to get lots of practice. Get lots of experience. Try lots of styles and techniques and tattoo lots of different body parts. How else will she learn to work her way around the curves and angles of shoulders, ankles and ribs? How else will she learn how colors work together, how to make lines thick or thin, and how to shade and highlight a design? And ultimately, how will she know how to advise clients who are not entirely clear on what they want?

Once you learn how to do something – as a tattoo artist or as a speaker – you don't stop doing it. You keep doing it so you can stay fresh and up-to-date when you're asked to do it again.

A tattoo artist must understand the technology, tools, and equipment associated with tattooing.

Tattoo artists are responsible for knowing how their machines, their needles, and their inks work. They are responsible for understanding hygienic practices, sterilization, and proper disposal of hazardous waste, and for keeping on hand the equipment and supplies necessary to achieve a safe and clean environment. They need to know how to create and apply stencils from designs and how to make those stencils fit the body parts they're meant for. And they need to have a system for setting up their station so they're always ready for the next appointment. A tattoo artist will use all the tools at his disposal to do the best work possible.

A speaker also has tools of the trade, whether it's PowerPoint and a projector, or her own method of using notes and a timer. A speaker may use a microphone, a prop, some toys, a video camera, a presentation remote, a texting app, or a noisemaker. The best speakers know how to incorporate the right tools at the right time to make their presentations most effective for the audience, and they also know to test everything in advance to make sure it's working. (Download my Presentation Tools checklist at www.coachlisab.com/pfh-form.html.)

A tattoo artist must have faith in her abilities and not let fear hold her back.

Ultimately, a tattoo artist is going to embed a design in someone's skin, creating a permanent work of body art. There is no going back once the process has begun, although a client can end a tattoo if he's not happy with it. But whatever has been drawn is there forever. Talk about pressure!

A tattoo artist must trust in her gut that she knows what she's doing, that she's well-prepared, and that she's offering the client a piece of art that's memorable and special – even though she causes pain in giving it!

I'll leave you with this quote from tattoo artist Justin Holcombe, his answer to the question, "What essential skills are required?"

"The No. 1 thing in tattooing is confidence, because it's permanent. Most people say that would be intimidating to know that that's going to be on someone forever and I don't want to mess it up. That's why you try to get your friends to get tattoos so you can use them as pincushions or guinea pigs and you try to expand your horizons as an artist. Confidence and knowing that if you apply the proper techniques...you should feel confident that it's gonna come out OK."

• •

SELF-REFLECTION

Who could you ask to be your guinea pigs
so you get proper speaking practice?

• •

3. IMPROVE YOUR PRESENTATION WITH A STRONG OPENING

"Why didn't I lose that 20 pounds?"
Robert Stromberg accepting the Academy Award
for Art Direction for *Alice in Wonderland*

An Academy Award winner has 45 seconds to speak, and less flexibility to go over that time as the evening wears on and the show starts to run long. Why waste time with apologies and fillers? A well-prepared opening allows a speaker to jump right into the speech without wasting precious seconds.

At so many awards shows, very few of the winners get right into their speeches without several seconds of "Wow!", "Holy cow!", "Oh my gosh!", "Is this real?", "This is unbelievable!", and similar exclamations of surprise.

I'm not saying an outburst of emotion is inappropriate for this type of speech (that would make me pretty cold-hearted, wouldn't it?), but there is often so much time-wasting that speakers frequently get the "goodbye music" while they're still in the middle of their speeches. I'm sure that, for many of the award recipients, these outbursts are used to kill some time while they gather their thoughts and their breath and try to remember what they were going to say. But they're time-wasters nonetheless.

Beyond the outburst of emotion which, when brief, is acceptable, I have another theory about some of the more extended expressions of disbelief.

Is it possible that some winners actually play up their surprise in fear of coming across as egotistical? After all, if you just walk up, keep your cool, and start talking, you might look as though you expected to win all along. And that would be bad, right? Some of the winners seem genuinely surprised, while others seem to be putting on a big show.

I can't pretend to understand what's going through the nominees' heads as they prepare their speeches, wait for their names to be called, and then take the stage upon winning, all the while worrying about saying the right thing and dealing with Hollywood politics. But there is an awful lot of time-wasting on stage that could very easily be avoided.

Here's just one example of how taking out the fillers can make a huge difference in the opening punch of a speech.

David Seidler (winner for Original Screenplay for *The King's Speech*) gave one of the best awards speeches I've seen. And it could have been even better with this one tweak:

Instead of beginning with "The writer's speech. This is terrifying...." he could have left that out and started with his next line: "My father always said to me I'd be a late bloomer." It got a huge laugh, as Seidler was 73 years old at the time of the event. What a way to kick off a speech!

That being said, here are some award-acceptance openings that I found effective for their humor or thoughtfulness. While they still may have been time-killers, they were much better than the "Holy cow" extended fillers.

"I should have gotten a haircut." ~ Luke Matheny (sporting an enormous pouf of hair), accepting the Oscar for Best Live Action Short

"Forgive me. I must start by pointing out that three years after our horrific financial crisis caused by massive fraud, not a single financial executive has gone to jail. And that's wrong." ~ Charles Ferguson, Best Documentary for "Inside Job"

"It feels like that top is still spinning." ~ Paul Franklin, Visual Effects for "Inception"

"I have a feeling my career's just peaked." ~ Colin Firth, accepting the

Oscar for Best Actor. His entire speech was a winner, one of the few that night. His warning of "stirrings somewhere in the upper abdominals which are threatening to form themselves into dance moves" had a touch of absurdity about it while creating a humorous mental image.

"I'm very grateful for this, and surprised. My percentages aren't great. I've been nominated 20 times and this is the 2nd time I've won." ~ Randy Newman, Best Original Song for "Toy Story 3." He went on to explain, in his entertaining speech, how nominees were instructed not to take out a list of names to read, because it doesn't make good TV: "I just have to thank these people. I don't want to. I want to be good television so badly."

· ·

SELF-REFLECTION
How can your presentation opening rise to the occasion?

· ·

4. IS YOUR PRESENTATION LIKE A FLEA MARKET?

When I manage to get my butt off the couch for my three-mile walk on a Tuesday or Thursday, I often take a shortcut through a local swap meet.

Swap meets and flea markets are so fascinating; you never know what you'll find around each corner or how useful an item will be. On one table, there are antique lamps. On another, outdated computer peripherals. On the next table, you'll find baby clothes or a strange montage of chipped plate, smoke alarm, and bike tire pump.

Wandering around flea markets is fun because digging for the best finds is the whole point of going.

Presentations, on the other hand, should be organized, clear and cohesive,

and should not force your audiences to meander from idea to idea, wondering where you're going and what your point might be.
I've seen many speakers mush together several previous presentations. They're like the junk store or flea market of presentations, except that your audience doesn't want to have to dig through the mess to find the treasure.

Have you ever sat down to create a new presentation for a meeting or conference and decided that you had all the information you needed in several previous PowerPoint slideshows? So you opened them all up and started cutting and pasting slides from the previous presentations into a new one?

Previous presentations may very well have all the information you need to create your new presentation. But that doesn't mean you can just toss a bunch of old slides into a new slideshow and have a well-organized presentation that makes sense to anyone but you. You can't just take three slideshows and meld them together without creating a new structure that meets the needs of the new presentation.

Before you open those old presentations, before you look at any slides, sit down and structure your presentation the old-fashioned way.

1. What's your objective?
2. Who's your audience?
3. What do they need, want, and care about?
4. What do you want them to do as a result of your presentation?
5. What's your main message, and what are the three key points you want to make in order to get that message across?

Old-school. Start from scratch. Create the skeleton first.

Once you have a basic outline of your presentation, then, yes, you can feel free to insert slides from previous presentations that might fit. In fact, my presentations (one idea per slide, represented by one large image and a single sentence) are basically modular. If I decide I'm going to talk about fear and anxiety in a presentation, I can pull that whole module of, say, 9 slides, from another presentation. But only if it fits, only if it makes sense, and only if the look and style of the slides is consistent.

And I will still need to tweak some things. For example, if I'm talking to entrepreneurs rather than nonprofit employees, I will change slides that refer to building relationships with "donors and volunteers" to "customers and vendors." I will make sure color schemes and fonts are cohesive across all slides. I will substitute new activities, exercises, and discussions for any that worked for the previous audience but won't work now.

Having previous slideshows can be a great shortcut to a new presentation, and after all that work you've put in, you deserve to be able to use work you've already done.

But you do need to create a new outline each time a new presentation is required. Period. If you don't, and you decide that it's just easier and faster to carelessly throw together disparate slides from disparate presentations, your presentation will suffer.

You may think you're saving time by skipping this first crucial step. But really, you end up wasting your own time and your audience's time with a crappy and confusing presentation.

Don't make your audience hunt for the treasure. A presentation is not a flea market.

● ●

SELF-REFLECTION

How can you salvage a patchwork presentation?

● ●

5. DON'T OVERWORK YOUR PRESENTATION

If you've never made a pie, you might not know this, but overworking the dough for the crust makes a tough chewy texture rather than the light flaky texture we all prefer. If you overmix the dough when you're making, say, scones, the same thing happens: hard, dense, chewy scones instead of light, fluffy treats.

Overdoing it isn't just a problem with dough. Overcook a piece of fish, and the proteins seize up, making your fish rubbery, not flaky.

Overdo your exercise routine, and you end up too sore to go to the gym for days.

Overdo the celebration at a party, and you will feel pretty crummy the next day, whether from too much alcohol or too much food!

Which brings me back to overworking.

The typical speaker I coach is a procrastinator who throws the presentation together at the last minute. The "overworker," on the other hand, nitpicks it for months. He writes and rewrites, adjusting a few details each time. He practices every single day, several times a day.

What? This isn't a good thing? "But Lisa," you say, "I thought preparation was the holy grail of successful public speaking!"

Yes and no. You don't really know how any presentation is going to work until you get in front of an audience. And each audience is different. So at some point you just have to let go and trust that your presentation is all it can be and will come to life when you deliver it. Practice in front of a friend, coworker, or spouse and get feedback, but then just let go.

Let it percolate in your brain for a few days here and there without practicing it at all. Don't even look at it for a week. Then come back with fresh eyes.

Finish your presentation at least a full day before you deliver it. Don't change things at the last minute. If you do, you won't feel prepared; you won't have practiced the new material, and you may find yourself feeling lost or not resonating with your content.

Just like pie crust, your presentation should be worked on "just enough." What is "enough" will have to be determined by you. But practicing and changing it every single day for three months is just going to make you crazy. You'll never feel ready.

Lightly mix the ingredients. Gently fold them together. Then put your crust in the oven (that's your brain, in case the analogy isn't clear) and let it bake.

Walk away. And when you deliver it to the audience, it will be fresh, it will be tasty, and from that experience you'll learn what you need to do better next time.

• •

SELF-REFLECTION
How have you overworked a presentation
instead of letting it rest?

• •

6. WHAT'S HIDING IN YOUR PRESENTATION CLOSET?

I've been fantasizing about joining Project 333 (http://bemorewithless.com/project-333/). Project 333 is "the minimalist fashion challenge that invites you to dress with 33 items or less for 3 months."

What I love about this challenge is that, by going methodically through all of my clothing, not only will I put aside or get rid of things I'm not wearing, I will also gain a fresh appreciation for my wardrobe, which clothes look best on me, and which garments I might combine in a new way I hadn't tried before.

This is similar to how I approach a presentation that a client has been delivering for a while, when it needs some freshening up, tweaking, or revising.

One of the simplest ways to freshen up a presentation is to rearrange it.

For example, a client will come to me with a boring opening, a bunch of thank-yous, or no opening at all. I'll go through the presentation with her and find a great story, question, or activity a few minutes into the presentation. We'll take that nugget, bump it up to the very beginning of the presentation, and – presto change-o! – we've got an engaging, interesting new opening.

Sometimes we find the flow of the presentation doesn't quite work, and upon further analysis, we realize that there's actually a chronology or logical order to the presentation the speaker wasn't using. We'll shift the order of the main points, and now there's a pleasing flow that helps the audience follow the topic better.

It's like going through your closet and seeing your wardrobe with fresh eyes, whether by taking on a challenge on your own like Project 333 or by hiring an expert to help. If you choose to work with an image consultant, she'll put outfits together that you've never considered, and at the end of the session you'll have a whole new wardrobe without having to buy anything!

Poke around in your presentation and determine what can be rearranged. What would give it a better flow, a more organized structure, a stronger opening or closing? With a little extra effort, you'll end up with a presentation that has both substance and style.

· ·

SELF-REFLECTION
Sometimes you have everything you need in your presentation; you just need to rearrange it. What could you reorganize?

· ·

7. DON'T CRASH AND BURN

If you've ever watched a long-distance cycling race like the Tour de France, you've noticed that some riders are caught off guard by tight curves and hairpin turns along the route. They either go too fast and crash or lose time by taking unexpected turns too cautiously. The reason? Not all teams ride or drive the course in advance.

Here are two tweets by a rider about preparing for race days:

"Rode the course two times this morning, then will another time this afternoon before race time. Course is very hard...."

"Heading to check TTT course again. Had a great night sleep...."
(TTT stands for team time trial.)

Here are two tweets from another rider:

"Rode the course this morning, had lunch, now I'm in my room getting ready to go to the bus/start & ride the course again."

"Rode 4 laps of the TT today, getting to know it is important, deciding on gears to use isn't so easy." (TT stands for time trial.)

Not only are these riders and their teams checking the course once, but they're reviewing it multiple times.

Riders will note how tight the turns are, how bumpy or gravelly the road is, where there might be slippery painted lines on a rainy day. They will note when and where to brake and shift, how steep the ascents and descents are, and where there are flat areas and shade to recover. And they'll look for spots on the course where there are headwinds, tailwinds, or crosswinds. These notes allow them to plan their tactics and timing, and to be as fully prepared as possible.

Much like a competitive cyclist, you should check out your venue in advance.

As speakers, we're subjected to a wide range of venues, from classrooms to ballrooms to board rooms. I've spoken in a school cafeteria, in a living room, in a library, and in restaurants. Every location is different, with configurations, acoustics and furnishings that can improve or interfere with your audience's experience.

Why should you check your venue? To find out:

- Where the audience will sit and where you will stand

- What equipment is available and where it is, if permanently placed

- Whether the room can be heated or cooled appropriately

- Whether there are street noises, sounds from other rooms, echoes from lack of floor and wall coverings, or noise from air conditioning or fans

- Whether the room is the right size for the number of people attending

- Whether your equipment works with the equipment being provided (computers, projectors, sound systems)

- Where tables can be placed to put your notes, props, water, products for sale, etc.

- What the lighting is like and where it's focused

- Whether the doors slam or close quietly when people come in late (you might need to tape the door latches flat)

And more!

Don't crash and burn because you didn't bother to check a new venue thoroughly.

• •
SELF-REFLECTION
What do you look for when you check your venues?
• •

8. TO REAP THE BENEFITS, YOU HAVE TO PUT IN THE WORK

I love cooking, and I love food (you'll notice a lot of food references in this book). I fell in love with cooking when I was a teenager, and since that time, I've collected hundreds of cookbooks and read them like novels, cover to cover. I also read books, magazines, and food blogs, and watch shows on the science of food and cooking.

And because I want to get better at cooking, of course, I cook! This is how I've learned what flavors and textures go together, how to make things brown and crispy or light and fluffy, why some dishes can't be frozen, and lots of other important bits and pieces of information.

It always surprises and disturbs me when I read the comments below a recipe online where someone asks what seems like a ridiculous question. For example: "I don't like cumin. What spice can I use instead?" *Um, it's cumin. If you don't like the taste of cumin, you don't want this recipe.* Or "Can I substitute yeast for baking powder?" ***What?***

If you want to be a better cook, you need to study, but you also need to put that learning into practice. How else will you know that vinegar curdles milk or that using cake flour to make bread will lead to failure?

But maybe you don't cook. Maybe you want to get better at belly dancing or putting on eye makeup or lowering your golf score. Maybe if you could improve your problem-solving skills or your ability to analyze spreadsheets at work, you could even be rewarded through a raise or promotion.

Now, let's say you want to be a better speaker (and I believe you do, because you're reading this book).

Here are some of the reasons my clients have given for why they want to be better at public speaking:

1. To open up more opportunities at work by taking on greater responsibilities
2. To build reputation and visibility in their field
3. To stop dreading requests to speak by dealing with speaking anxiety
4. To have a unique voice and be heard, both at work and in personal life
5. To be more effective at expressing themselves
6. To build confidence, self-esteem, and self-respect
7. To have a marketable skill when changing jobs or starting a business

There are a lot of reasons that a person would want to improve their speaking skills, which mostly tend to boil down to:

- Money

- Reputation

- Confidence

- Service

These are pretty worthwhile and pragmatic goals. **But you'll never reach these goals or reap the benefits without practice.**

One of the most difficult habits to change for speakers (especially for those of you who speak occasionally as part of your job or for community events) is the habit of not practicing, or waiting until the last minute to practice a presentation.

I hear the argument, "I don't have time," more than any other argument against practicing.

You explain that you have too much other work to get done. Or that you have kids to pick up, a volunteer meeting to attend, and errands to run. Yet – somehow – you manage to make time to get your other work done, watch your favorite TV show, meet a friend for drinks, and get a manicure. **And** check Facebook eleven times a day.

If you don't **want** to practice, that's your choice. But be honest about it. Not to me – to yourself.

Realize that you are making choices about how you spend your time. Realize that you are choosing what you prioritize as important.

If you want to be a better speaker, for any of the reasons listed above and more, figure out how to prioritize your time to make practice a part of every presentation you create.

Make the choice to fit it into your schedule, just like you fit in the belly dance class, the golf game, and the extra time going over the spreadsheets.

It's pretty rare in this life to get something for nothing. Success comes from hard work. Hard work includes practicing your skills so you get better at whatever it is you choose – in this case, public speaking.

No more excuses. No more arguments. Make the time. You will be rewarded.

• •

SELF-REFLECTION
Where can you find time in your daily schedule
to prioritize practicing your next presentation?

• •

9. LESSONS FROM DRIVING: DON'T BE A MECHANICAL SPEAKER

Do you remember what it was like when you were learning how to drive? There were so many things to pay attention to, so many details.

Where do I put my hands and my feet? When is it too soon or too late to press the brake pedal? How much pressure do I put on the gas? How exactly can I keep my eyes on the road if I'm also trying to look into two rear-view mirrors? And how exactly do I adjust the radio while keeping both hands on the wheel?

I remember scraping against a pole in a narrow driveway because I just didn't have a concept of how wide my mom's car was!
When you're learning, every move is a conscious one. It can be overwhelming and even scary – especially when you're on the road in a 3,500-pound vehicle, trying to follow the rules of the road, drive the speed limit, change lanes, not crash into anything, and not get a ticket!

Now, think about what it's like for you after having been driving for 30 or 40 years.

Most of what we do is completely unconscious. It's just natural to move our feet, hands, and eyes simultaneously in the practice of braking, accelerating, entering traffic, avoiding a raccoon crossing the road, taking a call on Bluetooth, and a million other things we do every day. In fact, I imagine that all of us have had that experience where we're **so** much on autopilot that we get to a place and don't even know how we got there.

When you're a newbie to speaking, it's hard to put all the pieces together and make your body and mind cooperate and run smoothly when your brain is doing this:

What did I just say?

Look at the left side of the room.

Smile.

It's hot in here.

Am I pacing? Stop pacing.

Stop fiddling with the remote.

What comes next? What comes after that?

Push the button for the next slide.

I'm running behind. Should my activity take five minutes or three?

That person's not paying attention. How do I get her attention?

Slow down.

It's cold in here.

Uh oh, crutch phrase.

I need a drink of water.

Look at the right side of the room.

What was the name of the guy who asked that question before?

Why did I wear these shoes?

Increase volume.

Was that clear? Maybe I should explain it again.

Speed up.

Decrease volume.

The more you practice speaking in front of an audience, the more automatic these tasks will become. You'll just know what to do without thinking about it.

As a speaker, you should aim for somewhere between ultra-conscious and ultra-autopilot.

If you have to consciously think about every motion, every facial expression, every story, you come across as wooden, rigid, or staged.

However, if you deliver every presentation on autopilot, then you lack attention and presence, and you lose your connection to the audience.

Both extremes put you into a mechanical mode that your participants can see and feel, making for an uncomfortable audience experience, to say the least.
How do you develop this speaking approach that's conscious but not too self-conscious and autopilot but not in the clouds?

One thing: Practice.

Get in front of audiences every chance you get. Speaking to lots of audiences helps you get over the self-conscious over-awareness of everything your body and mind are doing.

Speaking to lots of audiences also allows you to get used to being in the moment and getting used to going with the flow of unexpected conversations and relationships that arise with each new group.

I certainly don't want to go back to the old days of having to think about every single thing my body is doing when I'm on stage. But I don't want to become so complacent about speaking that I don't even connect with my audiences.

· ·

· ·

10. YOU CAN'T HARVEST UNTIL YOU CULTIVATE

A couple of years ago, my husband and I bought two blueberry bushes, and I was thrilled! I had suddenly "discovered" blueberries at the age of 48 after never having liked them. I came across some delicious organic berries at a farm stand, and I was sold.

Besides the one berry that was on the plant when we bought it, though, it took forever to harvest any blueberries. Why? Well, the bush hadn't been planted. Why not? The ground hadn't been cultivated.

See, my husband is our gardener, and he had a lot of other plants to tend to, so he hadn't gotten around to getting the soil ready for the berry bushes. Once the ground was cultivated, he could plant the bushes, and then finally we would have blueberries.

It's the same with speaking preparation.

How much time do you spend getting ready to get ready to get ready (as a client confessed to me recently)?

You don't harvest because you haven't planted. You don't plant because you haven't cultivated.

You know you need to add speaking to your marketing mix. You know that speaking is one of the best ways to get people to know, like, and trust you. You know speaking is one of the best ways to grow your visibility and credibility, which results in more clients and customers – aka your "harvest."

But you're not harvesting. You're not reaping the rewards of speaking because you haven't cultivated your skills and built your confidence.

What are you waiting for? Are you waiting to get a speaking engagement on your calendar, and **then** you'll start cultivating?

Too late.

If you want to master the art of speaking and using speaking to grow your business, or even if you want to stop dreading speaking enough to **get** a speaking engagement on your calendar, you need to start cultivating. Now.

When that speaking engagement comes your way – and it will – you need to be ready. You don't want to start working on your skills and your confidence two weeks before the presentation, because you won't be ready, no matter what fantasies you have about being a quick study.

What exactly do you need to work on before that date comes? Maybe you still need to figure out the best way to structure your presentation. Maybe you've created the presentation but don't know how to use audience engagement techniques. Maybe you know how to engage the audience but your call to action isn't clear enough. Maybe your opening is dull and your closing is forgettable.

But you won't know this unless you start actively working on a presentation, getting feedback from colleagues or a professional coach, videotaping yourself, and practicing.

Start **now**, so that when the time comes, you'll have the skills and you'll have the confidence. So that when you get on stage in front of that group that has so much potential to hire you, buy your products, and tell the world about you, you won't disappoint them with a mediocre and forgettable experience.

●●

SELF-REFLECTION
Are you getting ready to get ready to get ready?
How will you break that cycle?

●●

11. GOOD THINGS TAKE TIME

While shopping at Trader Joe's, I noticed a bright, colorful greeting card on the shelf above the chocolate-covered almonds. I had been in the process of redecorating my office, and not only were the colors perfect, but the message – "Good things take time" – was even better.

Granted, maybe not **all** good things take time. I mean, a quick summer salad of ripe tomatoes, fresh burrata cheese, and a drizzle of olive oil takes about five minutes, but it's delicious.

And I'm sure you've been struck by inspiration before, where instead of struggling with a solution for weeks, the idea came to you instantly – in the shower – and you were able to make a problem go away almost as soon as it arose.

But let's also say, for the sake of argument, that a masterpiece painting or a well-made garment is going to take more time to create than a quick sketch or a sweatshop T-shirt. Or that a special holiday meal for guests is going to take longer to make than a Taco Bell bean burrito. A classic novel might take years to complete. The brick house that's wolf-proof ("I'll huff and I'll puff and I'll blow the house in") might be more appealing to live in than the one that's built of straw.

The good news is that you don't have to spend years creating your top-notch presentation (although if you're a highly paid keynote speaker, you may spend years refining and improving it).

But I'm afraid that it's going to take longer than a few minutes. Longer than a few days. And if that's all the time you're spending on crafting your presentation, don't expect massive results from it. Don't expect lots of clients, lots of referrals, or lots of sales.

What's "top-notch?"

- A top-notch presentation takes into account the audience's interests and desires. Your job is to serve the audience. You can't serve them if you don't know them. So first, do your research. This might mean talking to the organizer or sending out a survey to the participants in advance, or both. Either way, this phase may take days to weeks to complete.

- Then, when you know what they need, want, and care about, you'll start determining what your core message is and how your core points will deliver and illustrate your message. Add another week or so for this. (I'm guessing you don't have a full eight hours every day to work on your presentation, and you're doing these things in between your other work responsibilities.)

- Then, when you have the skeleton of your core message, flesh it out with stories, activities, questions, examples, analogies, and discussion. If you're experienced, this might take a week; otherwise, give it more time.

- If you're using slides, start to look for images that illustrate your points. (No, you're not going to load up your slides with bullets. I said "top-notch" presentation, not "put me to sleep" presentation.) This part is very time-consuming if you want to find the right images that engage your audience, make them think, trigger their emotions, and help you express exactly what you want to say.

🦟 Then practice. And I don't mean practice in your head. I mean, practice out loud, standing up, running through the entire presentation several times. Or many times, depending on how well you already know your material, how confident you are in your delivery, and how regularly you speak in front of an audience. This will take at least a week. (You'll find a download for an easy timeline to prepare your presentation on my website here...)

This nutshell version of preparing a presentation takes, conservatively estimated, five to six weeks. An experienced speaker might take less time; a newbie might need to stretch this out a bit.

Think about this timeline the next time you put a presentation on your calendar. Give yourself **more** than the amount of time you think you'll need. Think of all the other work duties, distractions, and procrastination that will interfere with getting this presentation done.
Think about the time you'll need for clarifying and confirming your audience's needs, your message, your structure, your delivery, your engagement activities, and your practice time.

If you're not giving yourself at least a month to prepare, you're shortchanging yourself and your audience, and you can't expect your presentations to be "good," much less "great."

• •

SELF-REFLECTION
*How much time are you giving yourself
to create a great presentation?*

• •

2 EXUDE CONFIDENCE

Many would-be speakers know they have the knowledge, the expertise, and the message. What they're missing is the confidence to stand up in front of an audience and share that message.

Lack of confidence is one of the biggest concerns holding back people who are smart, powerful, well-informed, insightful, and interesting, and who have something valuable and meaningful to share with the world.

Audiences – and people in general – are drawn to a person who shows confidence. We all know that we need to have confidence as speakers. But what is this magical thing called confidence, and where does it come from?

A confident speaker exudes positive energy that feeds and excites the audience. A confident speaker comes across as strong and authoritative, but not intimidating. A confident speaker appears relaxed but energetic, positive but not contrived, and knowledgeable but not arrogant, with good posture, clear eye contact, and decisive movements. Wow! That's a lot to live up to.

And the fact is, when you're able to accomplish these things, you gain more than just confidence, right? You gain the ability to draw people to you, to influence people, and to make a bigger impact in the world.

Confidence is both mental and physical. It's both internal and external. It's the positive way you perceive yourself, and it's the way your body projects that positive self-image.

In this section, look for lessons for speakers using examples from a runner, from Emmy award winners, and a singer who's not a singer.

12. PRESSURE TO PERFORM

A runner friend recently told me that when he turns the last corner in a race and starts heading toward the finish line, he starts to panic and wants to stop running. Seeing all the people watching and cheering makes him feel extremely anxious. The expectation! The pressure! Sound familiar?

Performance anxiety certainly affects speakers and athletes in similar ways. It never occurred to me, though, that crossing the finish line would create as much anxiety as crossing the starting line – I guess because I'm not a runner!

My friend also mentioned that there's an expectation that a runner will sprint the last few yards before the finish line, which also adds pressure.

However, he pointed out that the additional adrenaline stirred up by the crowd and perceived pressure actually propels him to finish the race, sprint and all.

The speaker's audience and the athlete's audience are also similar. Look at that cheering crowd at the finish line. What are they yelling? "Go!" "You can do it!" "Good job!" "Keep going!" And other supportive, encouraging things.

Okay, so the speaker's audience isn't yelling, "You can do it!" but they are thinking it! Yes they are. Just imagine for a moment that you're the person in the audience. You're hoping the speaker does well. You're hoping to learn something new. You're even hoping to be entertained a little. It's unlikely that you're sitting there thinking, "I hope she falls on her face."

The crowd at the finish line isn't thinking that, either. And anyway, what would happen if you fell (literally as a runner or figuratively as a speaker)? Would people laugh at you? Of course not. Would they deem you a failure? No. They would feel concerned, want to know that you're okay, and would encourage you to get up and keep going. Because we're all human, and we can all relate to falling down.

Speakers and athletes who learn to channel that adrenaline and use it find that manageable anxiety is helpful to them in achieving their goal. Also, by perceiving the audience as supportive instead of hostile, they retrain their brains to expect positive results in their endeavors.

● ●

SELF-REFLECTION
How can you reduce the pressure you feel onstage?

● ●

13. YOU'RE GOOD ENOUGH AS YOU ARE

A coach who teaches courses on financial freedom was once talking about how our brains are wired to want more of the things that make us feel good, but unfortunately, we sometimes can't stop ourselves wanting more and more and more. This causes us to overspend, thinking that if having "some" stuff makes us happy, having "more" stuff will make us even happier. She calls this "the gremlins of moreness."

I see much the same thing with my clients, except they think the magic bullet is "becoming" more, not buying more. They want to nail their presentations and become charismatic idols on stage.

I met with a client recently who had next to no speaking experience on his current topic. This is a fairly typical situation, where a client comes to me because he has expertise in another area, but is now required by his job to speak on a topic that is new to him.

All the confidence that this person used to have has gone out the window, replaced by anxiety and self-doubt.

After talking to this client and listening to him run through the outline of his presentation, the first thing I told him was that he came across as warm, friendly, approachable, and likable, and that this was going to be a huge factor in his success.

The surprise in his voice saddened me. He told me that no one had ever told him that, even in his previous speaking training. It made him feel so much better to know that **just being him** was going to be a benefit to his speaking. That **just being him** was a good enough place to start.

I find that speakers worry so much about the techniques, the words, their physical appearance, the "ums," the quiver in their voice, and the potential for mistakes, that they overlook the major factor of embracing who they are as a person and just connecting with the audience from that place.

I'm not saying that speaking skills aren't important – if that were true, I wouldn't have a job. You still have to learn how to develop and structure an effective presentation and deliver it successfully in a way your audience can understand, remember and use.

But no amount of skills and polish can overcome your own negative (or even shaky) perception of yourself.

If you feel that you're not good enough as you are, as a person, that insecurity is going to ooze out all over your presentation: in your posture, in your voice, in your facial expressions, in your movements.

You may not be an expert on your topic; your boss may be pushing you to speak on something you know little about. You may have a long way to go and a lot to learn. It happens all the time.

The point is: That's okay. You'll get it eventually. You'll keep learning (as we all do), and one day you'll have no qualms whatsoever about standing up and addressing that topic.

But right now, be secure in the knowledge that you are good enough as you are. No amount of "becoming" or "moreness" will help you make real connection with real people.

Connect like you would with a good friend or beloved family member. "You're good enough, you're smart enough, and doggone it, people like you." The rest will fall into place, but for now, start there.

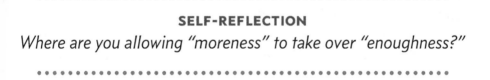

SELF-REFLECTION

Where are you allowing "moreness" to take over "enoughness?"

14. DON'T LET THE CONFIDENCE-SUCKERS GET YOU DOWN

At the Emmys a few years back, there was a similar thread running through several of the winners' speeches.

Jim Parsons, upon winning his award for "Big Bang Theory," said, "I was assured by many people in my life that this wasn't happening."

Julian Fellowes, recipient of the award for Outstanding Writing for a Miniseries, Movie or Dramatic Special, for his series "Downton Abbey," opened his speech:

"When we were in the hotel a bit earlier, my wife said to me, 'I think we should relax and enjoy the evening because I don't think we're going to win."

There was at least one other speech that started this way, but by that point I was too depressed to pay attention.

There are a lot of people in the entertainment industry who are superstitious and won't write speeches when nominated, for fear of "jinxing" their chances. If you watch the Emmys, you've seen plenty of these, who winners fumbled through their words, forgetting who to acknowledge and generally giving messy speeches.

But there's also another kind of "jinxing." It's when your colleagues, family, or friends don't give you the credit you deserve. Every performer, director, writer, musician, or other contributor to a TV show who has been nominated deserved it. Is there any doubt? Out of all the shows and movies on TV, only five or so get chosen as the top nominees in each category. So why would Julian Fellowes' wife and the people surrounding Jim Parsons try to convince them otherwise? I'm sure the thought process goes something like this: "We're up against a lot of good contenders and veteran Emmy winners (and so forth), so why get our hopes up? Let's just have a good time and see what happens."

The truth is, being nervous on the night of the Emmys, for everyone except those who host and perform during the evening, is a luxury. Nominees aren't required to **do** anything but sit in their seat. If they win, there's a short speech to give. So if friends and family have knocked them down a peg, it's not like their performance is going to suffer as it might if they were being asked to put on a show themselves.

But those negative attitudes wear on a person. And the more other people tell you you don't deserve to win, or you won't do a good job, or there are so many others who are better than you, the more you start to believe it. The confidence you do have starts to trickle away. You begin to doubt yourself.

Most of us won't win awards for our speaking. We are in the trenches, aiming to persuade colleagues and coworkers, trying to sell products and services, promoting a cause, teaching students, or giving important information someone needs to do a job or improve their life. We are not hoping for or expecting prizes for what we do.

Our "prize" is getting the promotion, acquiring the client, or on a more mundane level, just knowing we did a good job and that someone's life or work is going to be a touch better because of what we said.

The last thing we need is someone telling us we're not good enough and we won't succeed.

Don't listen to these people in your life! Don't let them drain you of your enthusiasm. Don't let them suck out your self-confidence. They may tell you they "only want to help," but they are not helping. They are making themselves feel better by making you feel bad. They are preying on your confidence and positive energy because they don't have any.

To Jim Parsons and Julian Fellowes, and anyone else who doubted their win: You deserve it! And to my readers who doubt their abilities every day: You can do it!

●●●

SELF-REFLECTION
Are there confidence-suckers in your life?
Can you stop doubting yourself based on what others say?

●●●

15. MAGNIFY YOUR FLAWS: TRY PUBLIC SPEAKING!

I'm at that time in my life when I need to use a magnifying mirror to I put on makeup or pluck my eyebrows; my vision has caught up with my age! But when I see the enlarged pores, the broken veins and up-close-and-personal crow's feet around my eyes, I'm horrified.

It would be SO much nicer not to have to look into that mirror and face the reality of my aging skin.

Who likes to look at our own flaws – any kinds of flaws? Not me. And not most people. In fact, I have a theory that many people are reluctant to give presentations not just because of how the audience will judge them but because of how they'll judge themselves.

As a personal development tool, public speaking can't be beat. If you don't learn a few things about yourself from the process of building and delivering a presentation, you may be self-awareness-challenged.

Here's just a short list of lessons you'll learn about yourself when you start getting up in front of audiences:

Time management problems? They'll come to the forefront.

Organization issues? Your audience will notice.

Preparation not your strong suit? You'll be scrambling.

Perfectionist? You'll drive yourself crazy. (This is me, by the way.)

Lack patience? Your audience will suffer.

Pessimist? Murphy's Law is a self-fulfilling prophecy.

Afraid to take a risk? Your presentations will be safe and boring.

Pretentious/vain/arrogant? The audience will be glad to escape.

Or it could go like this:

Time management problems? You'll learn how to edit a presentation so it fits into the time you have.

Organization issues? You'll become better at structuring your flow so the audience gets it.

Preparation not your strong suit? You'll discover that the more you prepare, the less nervous you are.

Perfectionist? You'll learn to let go. (Ahhh, it feels so good.)

Lack patience? You'll begin to appreciate where the audience is coming from.

Pessimist? You'll find that things don't always go wrong, but when they do, you're ready.

Afraid to take a risk? You'll start to enjoy trying new things when you see the positive audience response.

Pretentious/vain/arrogant? I'd like to think that you'll see how connecting with an audience on a human, authentic level gives immense satisfaction and is a win-win situation for both of you. But you might never learn this if you cling to the idea that a presentation is all about you and how brilliant and successful you appear to the audience.

Oh well. Nobody's perfect.

• •

What have you learned about yourself from public speaking?

• •

16. YOU DESERVE TO SHINE

A friend and I were talking recently about not submitting proposals to our local TEDx event. We shared our disappointment in this missed opportunity. Reasons for not submitting included not feeling like we had anything of value to say, worrying about speaking in front of local friends and peers, and concern about not knowing how to properly deliver this style of presentation.

This was an opportunity to be heard and seen, to share our core messages with not just our local community but with everyone watching the TEDx livestream on that day and in its future incarnation on the internet.

Think for a moment about all the things you haven't done or tried because of fear of failing, fear of embarrassment, or fear of looking foolish.

Was there a job you should have applied for? A person you wanted to date? An adventure you turned down? A book proposal you never submitted? A food you never tried? An inspirational person you never met? A conference you didn't speak at? A competition you refused to enter?

Now think about how your life might have been enriched if you had just taken the risk. Did you miss out on the opportunity to create, build, struggle, innovate, travel, love, defy, grow, feel, and survive?

Are you afraid to strive? Are you afraid of new ideas? Are you afraid of criticism or suggestions or difficult conversations?

Do you spend your days avoiding perceived danger, not listening, avoiding all risk, covering your you-know-what, and staying safe in your unchanging, ungrowing world?

How does that feel? I'm guessing frustrating, suffocating, boring, lonely, bland, sad, or tedious.

Now, think for a moment about a time that you took a risk.

You asked out that person, you shared your idea with your boss, you took that trip by yourself. It wasn't easy, and it might have been really stressful. And maybe the person said no, or your boss had already had the idea. Didn't it feel a little bit good to push yourself anyway, to try something out of your comfort zone? And if you succeeded, wasn't that even more awesome?

Take a baby step. (I'll share one of mine in the next section.) Pick one thing that you really want to do. One thing that you fear, but that you know could be really rewarding if you accomplish it (maybe it's getting a speaking engagement on your calendar!). Just start now taking baby steps to achieve that goal.

It's not as safe as you think to avoid taking risks. Staying "safe" will chip away at the **you** you could be. It will beat you down. If you don't take the risk, you don't grow. You don't thrive. You don't shine. And you deserve to shine!

● ●

SELF-REFLECTION
What did you learn from a scary growth experience?

● ●

17. SURPRISE YOUR AUDIENCE — AND YOURSELF

I attended a local business event a few years ago, where one of the guest speakers sang a portion of the song "Over the Rainbow" during her talk – and completely took the audience by surprise.

I loved her chutzpah and her willingness to try something different to get our attention, even though she told me that she's not comfortable singing in front of an audience. She inspired me to include singing in one of my presentations – exactly because I'm uncomfortable with the idea.

I didn't know how it would happen, and I didn't want to plan anything for fear of being too nervous to pull it off.

So a few weeks later, I took a baby step. At the conclusion of one of the group exercises during my training, I discovered that several people in the room didn't know the song "Auld Lang Syne." If you don't know it either, it's the song many of us sing at midnight on New Year's Eve.

So I sang a line of it to jog their memory. Okay, it was only a line. It was no "Over the Rainbow." But I was pleased with myself that I said I was going to sing during a presentation and I did. And because it wasn't planned, I didn't have time to get nervous about it.

The irony here is that I used to sing in front of people all the time. I sang in choirs, I had leading roles in musicals, I sang in a quartet, a trio, and a duo, and I performed whenever I got the chance.

As I got older and got out of the habit, I became more self-conscious about singing in front of people. I won't even do karaoke. I'm no Celine Dion, but I can carry a tune and the dogs won't start howling.

So how exactly does this insidious thing happen to us over time, this discomfort with exposing ourselves and fear of taking a risk? Especially around things that we used to do with complete confidence?

Maybe John Lennon was right when he said, "Every child is an artist until he's told he's not an artist." (A version of this quote is attributed to Pablo Picasso.) The loss of our pride and joy in boldly sharing a drawing or painting is one of the most commonly shared woes of growing up.

I don't know, but I don't want to let it control me. So I'm going to do it again. I'm going to find another way to incorporate something uncomfortable into a presentation. Because it's a challenge for me, because it's unexpected for the audience, and because it adds an element of fun and spontaneity to a presentation.

• •

SELF-REFLECTION
What have you done lately to stretch the boundaries of your presentation comfort zone?

• •

18. REMEMBER YOUR COURAGE AND MOVE FORWARD

"Nervous about taking a risk? Just remember when you did something that really took guts. You'll discover that you've always had what it takes to do what you want."
— Certified Life Coach Gail Blanke —

Gail's point is a reminder that when you're facing a challenge or being held back by fear or uncertainty, remembering your life's defining moments (when you overcame adversity and used some deep inner strength) will help you move forward.

I talk to a lot of people who don't think they can "do" public speaking. They fear judgment, they fear being revealed as an impostor, they fear boring the audience, and on and on.

If they were to sit down for a few minutes and think about a time in their lives where they thought they couldn't do something but did it and succeeded – and found that inner courage – they might realize that they can do it – that they can do anything.

I'll share one of my defining moments as an example.

I was the brand-new training coordinator for a nonprofit organization and I was having a lot of trouble getting responses from my counterpart at a nearby college who was supposed to be partnering with us in a new training program. The seeds had been sown by my predecessor, but now I couldn't get her to return phone calls or emails. I was ready to give up on this partnership altogether, but I didn't have the authority to make that decision.

Finally, there was a breakthrough, and she came to a meeting with our top-level directors to hammer out the details of the contract. Everyone in the room knew that she had been unresponsive and difficult to work with for months, but it seemed that no one was going to address the issue.

I sat there in the meeting, realizing that I was going to have to say something. My heart started pounding, my mouth dried up, my palms started sweating, I could feel my face heating up, and I missed half of what was said due to the ringing in my ears. I couldn't believe that no one was going to say anything, and I was going to have to take the plunge. As the meeting started to wrap up, I spoke.

I stated that she had been unresponsive in the past and I needed reassurance that she would follow up on her part of the contract in the future. The room fell silent.

She replied, making excuses and defending herself, and I thought, "Great, I just opened my mouth for nothing, because she refuses to acknowledge that anything was wrong. And no one will back me up."

Then the executive director spoke authoritatively. He demanded that she take responsibility for following through, that she respond to emails or phone calls within 24 hours as was our policy for our staff, and that she respect our partnership by being reliable and considerate of the partners. He even karate-chopped his hand a few times, if you know what I mean.

She meekly agreed.

When the meeting was over, several directors came to me, shook my hand, and thanked me for bringing up the issue. It was a huge moment for me, standing up for myself and the organization, and discovering that everyone else was just as uncomfortable as I was confronting the issue. I was no longer the "new guy" after that, nor was I intimidated by the directors, as I realized that they trusted and supported me.

To this day, I carry that experience in my back pocket, a reminder of a time when I demonstrated courage and stood up for myself. Knowing that I was able to overcome intense anxiety about that situation and speak up when it was necessary is something I'll never forget.

SELF-REFLECTION
What are some of your defining or courageous moments? How have they moved you forward?

3 MAKE IT FUN

I'm going to put this right out here: Most of us take ourselves too seriously as speakers.

There are a lot of reasons for this, but most stem from insecurity and lack of confidence. Speakers take themselves too seriously out of fear: fear of taking risks, fear of looking stupid, fear of standing out and possibly drawing criticism to themselves.

Speakers who take themselves too seriously are all about playing it safe, not rocking the boat, not saying anything controversial, not making mistakes, and certainly not having fun.

As Ari Weinzweig, co-founder of Zingerman's Community of Businesses, says, "People who lack confidence, who are more afraid of making mistakes than they are of missing out on opportunities, are less likely to make exceptional, innovative leaps."

We think we have to be "professional," and "businesslike" in order to be taken seriously, and so we take ourselves too seriously. Which basically translates into dull, dreary, and boring. Yuck.

Here are the arguments I've heard against making presentations fun:

"I feel silly using toys, activities, or music in my presentation."

"My boss would never go for something he considers 'fluff.'"

"We have to do slides full of text and bullets because our clients don't take our presentations seriously without it."

I had a commenter on a blog post once say this: "I'm pretty sure that everyone would sign up to be more 'engaging.' More 'captivating.' More 'engrossing.' These all fit with a workplace setting. Now all that being said, **how** you do these stuffy businesslike things turns out to be exactly the same way that you'd be more fun. It's just that you don't use the 'f-word' and so you don't feel so silly about the whole thing."

Sorry, pal. I'm not talking about engaging, captivating, or engrossing. I'm talking about **fun**! Yes, I'm going there.

What if you were to have **fun** on stage? And what does having fun have to do with making exceptional and innovative leaps?

Fun is about creativity. Fun is about freedom. Fun is about not being afraid to fail. Fun is about making your ideas accessible to people in a way that sets you apart. Fun is about bringing the audience along on an adventure.

Fun is just one method of audience engagement, and I specifically chose to call this section "fun" instead of "engagement" for this reason: We are missing the fun.

One of my core training concepts is audience engagement, and there are plenty of ways we can engage our audience's emotions that aren't necessarily fun – telling heartfelt stories, dredging up their frustrations and anger about problems that need to be solved, or using shocking statistics and demonstrations that just plain freak people out.

But as I said, I believe we're missing the fun. The joy. The playfulness. This is why this section is about "fun."

Julia Child's standard advice to novice chefs was to "try new recipes, learn from your mistakes, be fearless, and above all have fun!"

Child took her work seriously, dedicating her life to learning about cooking and cuisine. But did you ever watch her TV show? She absolutely did not take **herself** seriously! And this is what allowed her to convey her vast knowledge to American casual cooks who were scared to death of "fancy" French recipes.

In this section, look for lessons for speakers using examples from an Olympic snafu, a drag queen, and NORAD.

19. TURNING A FAILURE INTO A WIN

If you watched the opening ceremony of the 2014 Winter Olympics, you'll remember that there was a snafu with the display of the Olympic rings, when an electronic snowflake that was supposed to expand into the fifth ring never opened.

I often write about elite and Olympic athletes who don't dwell on mistakes, but instead get up from a fall or crash and keep performing, sometimes going on to achieve even more than expected. Well, clearly, Olympic ceremony designer Konstantin Ernst has the same die-hard spirit.

In the closing ceremony at Sochi, a group of dancers wearing glittering costumes formed the shape of the Olympic rings. As four of the rings formed, one group of performers instead stayed in a small, tight circle for a few hilarious moments, parodying the opening night mishap. But unlike in the opening ceremony, the fifth ring finally expanded and joined the rest.

By incorporating his mistake and poking fun at what initially was probably embarrassing, Ernst demonstrated his sense of humor, his flexibility, his willingness to laugh at himself, and his ability to take a mistake and make something better out of it. He even showed up to the closing ceremony in a newly designed T-shirt sporting four Olympic rings and a snowflake.

A couple of years ago, I had a technology mishap – not quite on the scale of the Olympics, but still embarrassing. At one point during my training, I was going to show the audience a video of a three-minute speech, similar to the one I was teaching them how to create and deliver. But while the video showed up on the screen, there was no audio.

We brought in the A/V person, who started going through his checklist of tests, and I attempted to entertain and keep the audience engaged by asking questions and pretending to tap-dance across the front of the room.

We never got the audio to work, and I ended up giving everyone the link to watch on their own. People commented to me after the training that they admired how I handled the complication and that I modeled the opposite of freaking out. I demonstrated for them that humor and composure go a long way!

We're all going to experience bloopers on stage. For most of us, millions of people around the world won't be watching. But our ability to exhibit grace and resilience under pressure and a sense of humor, and to understand that we're all human, will go far to entertain and satisfy our audience – and perhaps give our presentation that extra luster that people will remember long after it's over.

• •

SELF-REFLECTION
How have you handled a presentation mishap with grace and humor?

• •

20. NO SUCH THING AS A DRY TOPIC

I've heard from my clients who are engineers, financial advisors, doctors, and scientists that their topics are dry and boring because their audiences want tons of data, and that there's no way to make their presentations interesting or fun.

They could not be more wrong.

A topic is dry when the writer or speaker makes it that way, period. Here's an example of the opposite approach from my high school geography textbook, *Geometry: Seeing, Doing, Understanding* by Harold R. Jacobs.

The book introduced two characters named Obtuse Ollie and Acute Alice. They would perform experiments that demonstrated the math problems we were trying to solve. The interaction of these two characters was just one example of the kind of humor and engagement that the book used.

The textbook used art by M.C. Escher, Peanuts® cartoons, games (including one from a 1917 paperback), graphic design, a measure from a musical piece by Bach, the image of a batter's swing, examples from history (Mount Vernon, a 17ᵗʰ century Persian plate, tapestries, a silver vase, a Peruvian rug), stories, and more.

I was never a top math student, but this class was one of my most enjoyable and most memorable – and not because of the teacher. This book made all the difference in my interest and ability to learn geometry.

I sat with a client once who was going to be giving a presentation on cloud computing, a technical topic for an audience new to the concept. Going through his slides, I noticed that he had a slide that spelled out the definition of cloud computing.

I suggested he interview people at the conference the day before his presentation and ask them what they thought "cloud computing" might mean. Then, in the presentation, he could use the more confusing or humorous responses as definitions of what cloud computing is **not**. That way, he could kick off the talk with some light humor to get the audience engaged before diving into the nitty gritty of the topic.

As a speaker, what stereotypes about your topic are you clinging to? That science can't be interesting? That finance is boring? That insurance puts people to sleep? You can change that. It just takes some creativity, some willingness to challenge the status quo, and, as always, your own interest in your topic.

You bring the energy. You bring the fun. You make it what you want it to be. I'll say it again – there is no such thing as a dry topic!

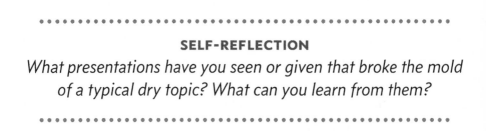

SELF-REFLECTION

What presentations have you seen or given that broke the mold of a typical dry topic? What can you learn from them?

21. FOUR LESSONS FOR SPEAKERS FROM BROADWAY

I got a message from a friend one day who had tickets to the show *Avenue Q* and couldn't use them. She asked if I wanted the tickets. Well, as a former theater major, an offer for free tickets to a touring Broadway show is something I do not turn down!

Of course, while I found it entertaining, original and funny, I also found some lessons for speakers! Here they are:

It's okay to have help.

In Avenue Q, the stars of the show are large puppets, handheld on stage by the actors who play them. The puppets, while technically the stars, would be useless without the bodies and voices of the actors. It takes a few minutes to get the hang of mentally integrating both the puppet actions and the actors' facial expressions and movement, but once it starts to work, it's seamless.

A lot of speakers have a fear of appearing fallible. They want to hide their notes or not use any. They fear making a mistake or having to deal with a technological problem, possibly revealing a flaw in the preparation of their presentation. If everything doesn't go exactly as planned, the presentation is a "failure" or "disaster."

Unless you're a magician, there's no need for elaborate illusions. Let go of your notions of perfection. So the audience sees that you have notes. As long as the notes aren't crippling the flow of your presentation or creating a distraction for you, who cares if they're sitting on the lectern off to the side? As long as you integrate your tools and don't blow your cool if something goes wrong, the audience will be fine with seeing the strings and gears of your presentation.

Visuals should be simple.

Avenue Q uses video screens at strategic times during the show to illustrate scenes and songs, as an educational tool in the same way that Sesame Street taught us that "C" is for cookie. For example, there is a song about schadenfreude, which is helpfully broken down for pronunciation on the monitor. In another scene, we see five illustrated nightstands on the monitor, and a countdown to "one night stand." (Get it?) And when

Princeton, the main character, forgets what he's looking for, the monitors drop down and remind us, with just the word "Purpose."

Never forget that you, the speaker, are the presentation. Your visuals enhance your presentation, but are **not** the presentation. If your PowerPoint was the presentation, you could email hard copies to everyone and tell them to stay home. Visuals can be helpful in illustrating your points, adding humor, demonstrating data, and more. But you are the focus and the center of attention. Don't let your visuals overwhelm you or the audience.

Use the element of surprise.

One of the songs in *Avenue Q* is titled, "Everyone's a Little Bit Racist." Another song says, "The more you love someone, the more you want to kill him."

Both of these songs have elements that might surprise and even shock the audience, because they're saying things that people often think, but would never say out loud.

How can you wake up your audience with a story, statistic, or activity that might use surprise or shock to help them learn something new or grasp a difficult concept? I wouldn't do this gratuitously; otherwise, your audience might end up feeling manipulated and confused or angry. But if there's a sincere or legitimate reason, go for it.

It's okay to be entertaining.

Okay, *Avenue Q* is a Broadway musical. It's supposed to be entertaining. But if you notice, many of the movies, TV shows, and plays we watch have a greater message, yet we are still entertained by them. In fact, it's the entertaining quality that allows us to more easily absorb the teaching. *Avenue Q*'s main message is that, while life is hard and there are no easy answers, everything – good and bad – is "only for now."

LUCY
For now we're healthy.

BRIAN
For now we're employed.

BAD IDEA BEARS
For now we're happy...

KATE MONSTER
If not overjoyed.

PRINCETON
And we'll accept the things we cannot avoid, for now...

As a speaker, you can pound your audience over the head with facts, figures, numbers, and charts. You can maintain a serious demeanor in the hopes of convincing the audience of the importance of your message. Or you can find ways to have some fun and make your presentation actually enjoyable to your audience while still making your points.

SELF-REFLECTION
What lessons about speaking have you found in surprising places?

22. ADD SOME FUN TO YOUR PRESENTATION WITH A SKIT

As my friend the fitness trainer set up her materials and then walked out of the meeting room to change clothes, our networking group settled into a low hum, chatting with each other and eating lunch. Imagine people's surprise when I stood up and exclaimed loudly, "What is taking Nicole so long?"

I went on, "Isn't it just like a trainer to always be late? I was really hoping to get in a workout today." Two others joined in on the complaining.

Of course, it was all part of a skit arranged by my colleague, who was going to be talking about how to choose the right personal trainer. She had asked a couple of us to kick off the skit while she was changing into her stylish rubberized sweat suit.

As I pulled on my sweatbands, I invited the other plants to join me, and we all began to stretch and talk about how unreliable trainers are.

At first, there was clear confusion and discomfort on the faces of our fellow attendees. Soon enough, though, the group clued in. One person exclaimed,, "I think this is part of the presentation!" And then the room relaxed and began to enjoy the silliness. The whole setup took about three minutes, before Nicole arrived back in the room with her whistle and her cell phone, playing the part of a stereotypical fitness trainer.

Bringing an unexpected element to your presentation is a great way to shake things up and get your audience on board with your message in a completely new way.

The initial discomfort only enhances the eventual realization that it's a gag and adds to the audience's enjoyment of the skit and final presentation.

• •

SELF-REFLECTION
Have you ever included a skit in your presentation? Could you?

• •

23. CAN YOU LAUGH AT YOURSELF?

A couple of years ago, I created a workshop called "Public Speaking for Awkward Dorks," with the explicit goal of making fun of my own goofiness onstage. My intention was to invite those who feel too "dorky" to be taken seriously as speakers to identify with me and my fellow dorks and goofballs, while learning actual tools to be successful onstage.

It was an effective promotion, as it turns out a **lot** of people feel like they have to hide their true weird selves onstage. Using self-deprecating humor opened the door to a human connection.

"Humor is a powerful weapon," says Jeff Nussbaum, a speechwriter who has worked for Al Gore and Joe Biden. "But to earn the right to wield it against others, you need to turn it against yourself first."

Why do we love a speaker who uses self-deprecating humor?

- It humanizes her.
- It makes her less threatening or intimidating.
- It defuses tension.
- It shows she doesn't take herself too seriously.
- It makes us laugh … and we love to laugh.

Self-deprecating humor allows us to be smart, funny, and confident, while also demonstrating modesty and humility about those qualities. After all, a person who uses self-deprecating humor has to be confident, or she wouldn't risk making fun of herself!

What is self-deprecating (or self-effacing) humor? It's simply making fun of yourself to get a laugh. It's different than flat-out putting yourself down in that you are doing it specifically as a joke, not as a serious statement.

Someone who's a master of self-deprecating humor is British comedian Eddie Izzard, especially when a joke bombs. One of my favorite bits is when he writes an imaginary "note to self" on his hand, reading it aloud to the audience:

"No one got that. Never do that piece again."

"Lost everyone. No one understands."

"No one ever gets that one."

"Where is that bit going?"

He's confident enough in his routine that he can actually make a joke about a joke that doesn't work. And then he moves on.

Here's another example of someone who used self-deprecating humor at all the right times:

"Thomas Jefferson once said, 'We should never judge a president by his age, only by his works.' And ever since he told me that, I stopped worrying." ~ former President Ronald Reagan

Reagan's former speechwriter, Doug Gamble, said, "It seems one of the personality traits we most value in others is a sense of humor. In fact, one of the worst things you can say about a person is that he doesn't have one."

However, you should be careful when using self-deprecating humor...

Use it too frequently and you begin to appear less confident.

Use it too emphatically and you look like you're fishing for compliments.

Use it to define a group and, even if you're part of that group, you'll make someone angry. (For example, the CEO of Netflix was blasted for making a facetious generalization about his fellow Americans being "self-absorbed." It didn't go over well.)

If you'd like to use more humor in your presentations, but aren't sure where to begin, try some self-deprecating humor. We all instinctively know how to do it and we do it all the time!

• •

SELF-REFLECTION
How have you used self-deprecating humor in a presentation?
How could you add it in the future?

• •

24. LESSONS FROM A DRAG QUEEN

Musical artists know that the best way to get the audience's engagement is to include them in the show, whether it's making them feel like a rock star when they sing along, creating a cheer or a chant that they can repeat, or bringing them onstage to participate.

I saw this in action one Saturday night at the Lips drag show in San Diego.

The emcee of the evening, Tootie, pulled out all the audience engagement tools. As emcee, it was her job to announce each performer and keep the evening on a tight schedule (there was a second seating after ours), but she also kept the audience engaged in between divas.

As bridal showers and birthday parties made up the bulk of the audience, these special audience members were incorporated into the show. They were invited onstage to share their name and the occasion they were celebrating, and each one got a photo with Tootie and another diva.

You can imagine this might go on for a while and become rather dreary. Who wants to see people you don't know onstage, looking embarrassed and repeating "It's my birthday" two dozen times?

But Tootie (who does this how many times a week?) managed to keep the experience lively and fun. She had a joke for every guest, and while some of her patter was canned, she was good at thinking on her feet and being in the moment.

There was also an activity that involved several brides-to-be joining Tootie onstage for a bridal "lesson." I won't go into detail, but the activity was funny without being humiliating. Hard to pull off sometimes in a sassy/ snarky environment like a drag club.

The most impressive part of the evening (from the audience engagement perspective) was the break between performers for what I'm going to call the "shot pitch." At this point in the evening, dinner and drinks were winding down and, unless they bought dessert, there would probably be no more money spent.

At this time, Tootie pitched some fruity and refreshing-sounding $3 shots, both alcoholic and nonalcoholic, to the crowd – and made them sound like a great deal. And then in a brilliant bit of salesmanship, she asked each table, one by one, to call out their order. Out of all the people in the room, I only heard two (small) tables call out "none."

Peer pressure! But approached in a way that the audience participated out of a sense of fun and camaraderie rather than angst or guilt. I wish more internet marketers and speakers understood upselling this well. Granted, most internet marketers are selling a product at the end of a mediocre and boring free teleseminar, not at the end of a boisterous dinner show.

But when audience members get involved, we all feel a little more part of the show. And when you feel like you're part of the show, the show is going to be that much more enjoyable and memorable. This is when your audience will say "yes" to you.

● ●

SELF-REFLECTION
What do you want them to say "yes" to?

● ●

25. NINE WAYS TO USE PROPS FOR MAXIMUM IMPACT

One of my former networking colleagues called himself the "electronic therapist." In the span of a ten-minute presentation at one of our meetings, he was able to pack in a ton of fun with a few well-placed props.

● He played with a Slinky, to represent a time when our entertainment needs were simple

● He put on a straw hat with a quote from monk and peace activist Thich Nhat Hanh painted on it, to represent "zen"

● He dumped a pile of remotes on the table to represent the pile of remotes we all have sitting on our coffee tables

● He produced a hilariously gigantic universal remote, in case we have trouble finding our regular remotes

There was so much going on in this presentation, there was no way the audience could lose interest. His style was deadpan, not silly, which made the use of props even more effective. His visual aids just kept coming, and his ability to understand the audience and our messy, complicated sound systems created an instant connection.

If you decide to use a prop, make sure it can be seen by everyone in the room, and don't bring it out until you're ready to use it; it's not nearly as much fun when the prop is already sitting there. Unusually big props are extra funny; so are unusually small ones if they're still big enough to be seen.

It's also important to practice with your props before you give the presentation, to make sure everything works into your timing properly and to make sure the demonstration flows smoothly. It's not funny if your prop doesn't work.

Props enhance your message, stimulate the audience, and can add a nice touch of humor without much effort. They can suggest a bigger picture. They can bring shock value. And they can contribute subtext. The visual impact of a prop is its power – your words are enhanced by props, and sometimes words are unnecessary when using props.

Here are nine ways you can incorporate props into your presentation, including some of my clients' examples that made a great impact in their presentations.

1. Take the audience on an emotional journey.

A speaker for a local nonprofit organization tells the story of a child who, at the age of six, went into foster care with nothing to her name but a few belongings stuffed into a black trash bag. The speaker brings such a bag – not even half full – onto the stage. When she lifts that bag into the air, you can imagine the few items of clothing, maybe a small doll or teddy bear, and the sadness of a child without a permanent home. It paints a picture more powerful than words alone.

2. Bring the world to your audience.

I watched a speaker prepare for his presentation a few years ago by putting on layers and layers of clothing. His intention was to take his audience on a trip through history, enhancing his talk by revealing costumes from different time periods as he peeled away the layers. Sure, you could throw some images up on the screen from different time periods. Or you could actually wear the clothing and bring the shapes, textures, and colors from another time right into the room where your audience can see it up close and personal.

4. Make sure your prop is relevant.

Larry Winget is a keynote speaker who calls himself the "Pitbull of Personal Development." He's known for his "prop humor." For example, he pulls out roadside signs that he's swiped (again, you can put it up on the screen, but a real-life prop can be much more effective) demonstrating his point that "people are idiots." Part of his talk includes suctioning a toilet plunger to his bald head. Whatever outrageous prop he pulls out, it's always tied to his message. Can you say the same?

5. Keep it simple.

The simpler it is to use and show your prop, the less distracting it will be to your audience. Like your slides, the prop isn't your presentation; it merely enhances your presentation. Depending on the size of your audience and how far away they are, your prop can be as simple as a book, a magazine, a phone, a vegetable, or a shoe. There's no need for elaborate props – unless you're, say, Gallagher. Or maybe you're a scientist and you're going to blow things up. Your prop should be able to make your point simply and without a lot of effort.

6. Keep it hidden.

Another local nonprofit speaker keeps his apron hidden under his shirt until the appropriate time in his speech. Then he rips open his shirt, à la Superman, and reveals it. It's a great moment that always makes the audience laugh. Props work best when they aren't seen until the right moment. The surprise factor is especially effective when you're using your prop for humor. Sometimes it isn't possible to keep your prop hidden, and when your prop is visible, just know that your audience is going to be distracted by curiosity. So if you're using a prop that can't be hidden, at least get to it sooner rather than later. Unless the anticipation is part of your intention. And then, well, let them stew!

7. Be absurd.

If you're using your prop for humor, consider going over the top. That is, if you want the audience to really get it, you might have to be a little larger than life. Here's an example: An old Saturday night sketch used a teeny-tiny cell phone to demonstrate how ahead of the curve the character Jeffrey was. When we see Jeffrey again, a few months later, this time he pulls out a huge 1980s "brick phone." When his employees make fun of him, he says, "Please. Big is the new small." The prop is more absurd because we've already seen the tiny phone. And it's absurd because it's bigger than just big. It's old, it's obsolete, it's ridiculous.

8. Help the audience feel the feeling.

In the documentary "Fat, Sick, and Nearly Dead," we watch Phil Staples, a morbidly obese truck driver, transform himself into a health-conscious and inspiring role model for other overweight people. Phil becomes so transformed emotionally and physically, he starts giving talks and sharing his story.

At one point, he lines up six bowling balls to show the audience how much weight he's lost. I don't know exactly how much those bowling balls weighed, but I can tell you that the thought of wearing those on my body every day, and the thought of trying to move and walk and sleep and sit with those attached to me, caused a strong emotional reaction.

I could almost **feel** that weight hanging off of me. It was more than an emotional response; it was a visceral one.

9. Be creative.

I have a lot of clients who come to me from fields like finance, insurance and engineering, who tell me that their topic is boring. They feel completely at a loss as to how to take numbers and data and charts and make their presentations interesting to their audience.

And they're making it way too hard on themselves.

Astronaut and former International Space Station Commander Colonel Chris Hadfield made many videos from space, explaining a variety of issues astronauts face. One of his videos was about why it's difficult to taste food in space. His props were simple but fun: treats and snacks that had been sent to the ISS by his fellow Canadians.

A final note: **Don't let your props throw you off.**

If you've never worked with props before, you might be surprised to discover that things don't always go as you envisioned it. Maybe it takes too long to get your prop out of its container. Maybe the prop is too small and the audience can't see it very well. Maybe your prop makes a big mess that you hadn't anticipated. Maybe your prop is awkward to hold or display.

Always practice your presentation with your props. Don't just imagine how they're going to fit in, but actually pull them out and use them while you're rehearsing. The more you practice with your props, the more naturally they'll fit into your presentation, and you'll have a better idea of how they're going to work in front of a live audience.

Think outside the box a bit on what kinds of props would help your audience grasp your message.

SELF-REFLECTION

How will you use props in your next presentation?

26. A PUBLIC SPEAKING LESSON FROM NORAD

Have you heard of NORAD? According to its website, North American Aerospace Defense Command is "a United States and Canada bi-national organization charged with the missions of aerospace warning and aerospace control for North America. Aerospace warning includes the monitoring of manmade objects in space, and the detection, validation, and warning of attack against North America whether by aircraft, missiles, or space vehicles, through mutual support arrangements with other commands."

Sounds pretty serious, huh? NORAD defends the airspace of North America, monitoring "a worldwide system of sensors designed to provide the commander and the leadership of Canada and the U.S. with an accurate picture of any aerospace or maritime threat."

Guess what else NORAD monitors? **Santa Claus.**

Starting on December 1st each year, the military organization's *NORAD Tracks Santa* site goes live, counting down the days until Christmas Eve, and then showing Santa's flight around the world. Santa trackers can speak to a live operator to inquire about Santa's whereabouts, can watch video and play games on the site, and can even use apps on their phones to make sure they don't miss a moment of Santa's journey.

Now, let me ask you this: If an organization as "important" and "serious" as NORAD can put up a Santa tracking website, can't you have a little fun in your presentations? If putting up a Santa tracking site doesn't ruin NORAD's reputation or credibility, how could having some fun with an audience ruin yours?

Stop taking yourself so seriously. Lighten up. Be a breath of fresh air for your audience, rather than a rigid, humorless, windbag presenter who promotes his own superiority and importance at the expense of his audience's enjoyment and engagement.

• •

SELF-REFLECTION
How do you make your audience smile?

• •

4 CREATE CONNECTION

"Only connect! That was the whole of her sermon. Only connect the prose and the passion, and both will be exalted, and human love will be seen at its height. Live in fragments no longer. Only connect, and the beast and the monk, robbed of the isolation that is life to either, will die."

E. M. Forster, *Howards End*

I love this statement: **only connect.** It is the crux of human relationships. And it is the crux of the speaker/audience relationship. You can have good material, perfect organization, and skilled delivery, but if you don't connect with the audience, something critical is missing.

I also find that connecting "the prose and the passion" to be critical for a speaker, both internally and externally.

Connecting the prose and the passion internally means we are whole and complete; we are not ruled by either logic or emotion, but give both their equal time and weight. We don't value one over the other but embrace the practicality and benefits of both.

Externally, this means using facts and words as skillfully as emotion and expressiveness in engaging and impacting the audience.

When I started what you might call my "speaking career," my job was to give presentations in high school classrooms.

My topic: Abuse in teen relationships, AKA domestic violence. Sounds fun, right? Just what every teenager is hoping a speaker will come to their class to talk about.

It was nerve-wracking to walk into a room where my audience was mandated to attend and where the subject matter was difficult and uncomfortable. And connection? I had no idea what that was.

I was terrified, and I was inexperienced. Sure, I had been performing on stages since junior high school and had a degree in theater. But this was totally different.

Why would they listen to me? I wasn't cool. I wasn't talking about something they wanted to learn. I expected them to act rude, bored, and mean. But it was my job, so I dutifully picked up the one-page presentation that someone else had written and started going to high schools.

But here's what I learned, pretty quickly: Connection is where it's at.

Connection doesn't magically happen in a vacuum. It requires a few elements to be present: Trust, respect, listening, humility, authenticity, flexibility, a willingness to be real, and a willingness to be outside of your comfort zone.

When I mastered the art of connection – with teenagers – I felt like a superhero! I felt like I could take on any audience. And I did!

It doesn't matter if you're speaking to students, engineers, scientists, entrepreneurs, nonprofit leaders, or specialty food retailers. Everyone wants to connect.

In this section, look for lessons for speakers using examples from a sleep-aid advertisement, a college president, and a cinnamon roll cake.

27. ARE YOU "SLEEP-PRESENTING"?

While reading a magazine in the waiting room at my doctor's office, I came across an ad for a popular sleep aid. I found some of the side effects to be, at minimum, disturbing:

- Driving a car (sleep-driving)

- Making and eating food

- Talking on the phone

- Having sex

- Sleep-walking

Makes you want to take this drug, huh?

However, you don't have to pop a pill to be a "sleep-presenter." Here are some signs you're sleep-walking through your presentation:

- You drone on about your topic, paying no attention to the shifting, shuffling, yawning boredom of the audience.

- You keep your eyes glued to the screen as you robotically advance your PowerPoint slides, reading each one verbatim.

- You give a one-sided lecture, failing to involve the audience by asking questions or encouraging interaction.

- You rhythmically rock back and forth behind the lectern, head down, reading from your notes.

- You give the exact same talk to every group, regardless of their needs, interests or background.

See, it's easy to sleep-present; you don't need a drug to achieve this. You only need to lack attentiveness and interest in your audience. Piece of cake!

● ●

SELF-REFLECTION

What other examples of "sleep-presenting" have you seen? How can you make sure this isn't you?

● ●

28. IS YOUR SPEECH TOO "SPEECHY"?

While coaching a client on a rehearsal dinner speech for her son's wedding, I noticed her reliance on expressions like "humble thanks," "heartfelt wishes," and "so honored to be here."

Why is it so easy to write in clichés? Why are so many speeches and presentations full of trite platitudes like these?

Because we've heard it all before. It's easy to write a speech in clichés, because after so many weddings, graduations, award banquets, and retirement dinners, it's the first thing that comes to mind; we've come to believe that **that's** what makes a speech a speech. That is: formal, flowery, wordy, grandiose and as far away from a natural conversation as you can get. Speechy.

Speechy is boring, it's unoriginal, and it causes your audience's eyes to glaze over. But how do you get away from it? How do you even recognize it?

My client told me that she didn't even realize the writing she was doing for her speech was so clichéd, and it makes sense, because clichés are almost invisible. They're quick little shortcuts we use to make a point without having to reinvent the wheel or, for that matter, think for ourselves.

If you want to know if your speech is speechy, ask yourself these questions:

1. Have I heard it before? And if the answer is yes, have I heard it a LOT?

Obviously, it's pretty hard to come up with completely original content for every presentation you give. Even professional writers are guilty of using the easy cliché. Every culture has expressions, idioms, and humor that will fold naturally into a speech, and you don't have to go crazy trying to avoid every possible common expression.

But if you hear it frequently, especially at formal occasions where people give speeches, try to think of some different words to express your thought.

2. Is this my voice?

You may want to give "heartfelt thanks" to all your guests, but is that really the way you would say it if you were hanging out having a beer together on the porch?

A speech can certainly be an opportunity for heartfelt thanks, but if those aren't words that would ever come out of your mouth on other occasions, then don't say them. A speech, like any other presentation, should still be conversational, natural, and authentic. You still want to come across as **you**.

3. Am I trying too hard?

A speaker sometimes sees a speech as an opportunity to use big words, too many words, too many adjectives, and too much pomp and circumstance. In an effort to impress the audience, the speaker spends days with the thesaurus, thinking up variations on "fabulous," "amazing," "wonderful," "tremendous" and "dynamic."

And oftentimes, the speaker puts untold pressure on himself to be pithy, profound, and poignant. (Oh yeah, you bet I used the thesaurus on that sentence). I still remember the high school valedictorian a few years back who used the word "jocularity" in his speech. Really? How many of the students in his class even knew what that word meant? I cringed, thinking of the work he'd put into that speech that only served to distance himself from his audience.

Keep it simple. Express your deep and sincere feelings in a way that's meaningful to you and your audience. Make jokes, name names, and kiss butts if you must. But do it in your own language, your own words, your own voice.

· ·

SELF-REFLECTION
*How could your language be more sincere and
less grandiose in your presentations?*

· ·

29. SEE, HEAR, AND TASTE YOUR AUDIENCE

*"When the mind is not present, we look and do not see;
we hear and do not understand; we eat and do not know
the taste of what we eat."*
— Confucius, *The Great Learning* —

Have you ever sat down to eat lunch and, because you were so busy doing other things on the computer or talking on the phone, you suddenly realized your food had vanished and you barely remembered eating it?

It's a common occurrence that we get so wrapped up in our thoughts that we're not aware of what's happening around us. We go about our day not seeing, not hearing and not tasting.

We do the same thing as speakers.

We can get so caught up in what's going on in our minds and bodies that we neglect to be in the moment with our audience.

There are usually about a million things going on in our heads as we stand up to speak. And along with all the logistical chatter, we're also obsessed with every physical aspect of nervousness: the flip-flopping stomach, the quivering voice, the gelatinous knees.

With all this going on, how can you possibly pay any attention to what you're saying, seeing, and hearing, and how your audience is responding?

First: Breathe and ground yourself. Grounding yourself literally means to connect your body to the ground and to feel physically connected to your body. As with any practice, the more you do it, the easier it gets. (You can find a grounding handout on my website www.coachlisab.com/pfh-form. html.)

This practice allows you to still feel and be aware of what's going on in your body and note what's going on in your head without being distracted by it all.

See
Once you're grounded and breathing, look at the audience. Focus on them as individuals. See faces instead of a blurry mass. Smile. Make eye contact.

Hear
Instead of just racing mindlessly to the end of your presentation as fast as you can, listen to yourself. Really hear what you're saying. Slow down enough that your mouth doesn't get ahead of your brain (this has been

known to happen to me), or ahead of your audience's brains.

When you hear what you're saying, you're less likely to lose your place or your train of thought. And you're more likely to speak clearly and articulately enough that your audience understands and grasps your message.

Taste

Like eating and not tasting, you might be observing the audience without noticing or internalizing their response. Are they listening? Are they paying attention? Are they engaged? Or are they looking out the window, playing on their phones, doodling in their notebooks?

Experience your audience. Notice their response to you, digest it, understand it, and do what you need to do to adjust your material or delivery to increase their engagement.

Being present is not easy. It requires focus and it requires awareness. It requires you to get out of your head and create a relationship with the audience.

But it's worth it for the increased rapport you build with your audience and for the greater enjoyment and comfort you will feel on stage.

• •

SELF-REFLECTION

How can you work on being more present with your audiences?

• •

30. FIVE PUBLIC SPEAKING LESSONS FROM A COLLEGE PRESIDENT

One of my networking groups held a dinner event with the new president of a local college as the guest speaker.

There had been turmoil at the school in the years prior to her arrival, and our community had been hoping for positive changes in conjunction with the change in leadership. This was a great opportunity to hear what was going on over there – and hopefully not just a sales pitch.

Right off the bat, I got a sense that she was going to be a great guest. Here are some of the techniques she used to connect with us that evening.

1. Networking
The president started off the evening by working her way around the room, introducing herself to the members of the group. Making friends with the audience and building a connection before you speak is such a simple tool for reducing speaking anxiety and getting comfortable with the room, but few speakers (besides politicians) think to do this.

2. Interaction
To begin her presentation, she paired off audience members and handed out a quiz. This is one of my all-time favorite activities, and again, I rarely see speakers engaging the audience at this level. It helps that she's a former teacher and easily applies teaching concepts to her talk, but it's not that hard for the average speaker to be a little more creative with engagement activities.

3. Anticipation
She gave the quiz up front, but instead of giving the answers all at once, she seeded answers throughout the presentation. That motivated us to focus as we listened and to see if we would get the answers correct (and

win a prize!). I'll tell you right now that, as a Santa Barbara native, I should have done much better on the quiz!

4. A light touch

The president not only took an interactive approach with the audience, but also made sure her facts and statistics were meaningful to the audience. Her slides were simple and clean, and unlike speakers who try to tell you everything about everything in a limited amount of time, she focused on the points she thought would actually interest the audience. The level of detail was interesting and appropriate, not overwhelming or mind-numbing. What a concept!

5. Inspiration

She told stories and expressed the achievements of her college and its students with authentic passion and enthusiasm. She was clearly inspired by her work, by the college and by our community, which was endearing to a local like me.

People who move to Santa Barbara from other cities and states are often not as invested in the culture as the locals (except for maybe those who are raising children here).

So I was pleasantly surprised to meet the new president and to hear not only of the amazing successes happening at the college, but also of her rapidly growing affection for the students, faculty and staff, and for the Santa Barbara community.

It was one of the most enjoyable presentations I have attended in a long time. It was informative, educational, fun, and inspiring. Not the kind of presentation I see every day, but the kind of presentation I help my clients aspire to!

• •

*Is there a speaker you've watched who gives you
exactly what you crave as an audience member?*

• •

31. DON'T LOSE YOURSELF IN THE ADORATION OF THE AUDIENCE

Here's a new expression I learned while watching the show "So You Think You Can Dance." One of the judges called a dancer's expression while performing a "hungry jazz face."

The judges' criticisms stemmed from their belief that the dancer was too busy playing to the audience and not demonstrating authenticity in his performance.

One judge said, "You are starting to become a little fake in your performance.... You have a magical quality and you love playing to the audience, but if you start faking your performance, that will get you into trouble with the viewers. Please be careful, and don't lose yourself in the adoration of the audience."

A couple of weeks later, I made note of the dancer's performances. No hungry jazz face here. He had paid attention to the judges' advice, had watched himself on video (as contestants all do each week), and had completely immersed himself in the performance, the character, and his relationship to his partner.

You might say that, as speakers, we don't have a partner, so the audience is our key focus. So what's wrong with playing to the audience?

When you speak, the audience is indeed your partner. As a speaker, you are in a unique position where you are performing for your audience while also partnering with them.

On the one hand, you must always be "on" for your audience. This means that, no matter what is going on with you internally, physically or mentally, your external demeanor is all for them. You smile, you interact, you engage them, you keep their attention, you maintain the dynamics in the room. (I don't care if you've got a temperature of 102 degrees – if you've committed to be there, you perform and bring energy and enthusiasm to the room or you suffer the consequences.)

On the other hand, you are also in an authentic relationship with the audience. You must bring your own emotion to the presentation in order to stimulate theirs, and you must be real with them, or they will disconnect from you. You must read them and understand where they're coming from. How are they reacting to you? Are you getting through? Are you reaching them? You won't make this connection if you are not authentic and heartfelt.

What concerned the judges in that dancer's first performance is that it was all entertainment and not enough engagement. He brought the energy but not the presence. He was more concerned with being liked by the audience than with making a real impact.

In the later dance number, he had the energy, the presence, and the authenticity and, while this number was not about his relationship with the audience, the audience couldn't look away or disconnect, because his performance was so compelling.

• •

*How can you be more real for your audiences? How can
you stop focusing on their adoration and instead
offer true inspiration and connection?*

• •

32. PERFECTION IS THE ENEMY OF AUTHENTICITY

I went to a book publishing workshop in 2007, thinking I would be writing a book soon. Ha.

The first speaker was very polished and professional. He had a warm, approachable personality, but I could tell that he had done this presentation many, many times before. He had a certain cadence in his speech that indicated that much of it was, if not memorized intentionally, memorized out of habit. There was great content, and he wasn't exactly robotic. Still, there was a disconnect for me emotionally.

The contrast between the first and second speaker was stark. The second speaker was excited. I don't mean excited like motivational speakers whose excitement is planned, measured, and contrived. I mean, she was jumping out of her skin excited. She could not wait to tell us about her unique method for writing a book. She was still beside herself for getting her own book published!

She was not a perfect speaker. She got off track sometimes with personal stories, her hair was disheveled and falling out of its clip, and her flip chart notes were a little hard to read due to her scribbly handwriting.

Which speaker do you think was my favorite? Yep, the one who couldn't hold back her enthusiasm for the topic. Passion is contagious – her passion for the process of writing and publishing a book made me feel excited, too. She was excited for us and the journey we were about to embark on together.

Sure, I also enjoyed the first presentation and came away with valuable information that I would be able to use. But I was inspired to **action** by the second presentation, and that's the mark of a successful presentation, whether the speaker says "uh" a few times or jangles some bracelets or forgets her place once or twice.

Don't try to be perfect. Focus on engaging the audience with your own passion, carrying them along on your wave of excitement. You can't help but succeed at motivating your audience to action.

If you feel you must memorize your talk and you must exhibit "perfection," I'm encouraging you to reveal yourself. Stop playing it safe. Be vulnerable. Be real. Take a risk. Be okay with mistakes.

Make connecting with your passion and connecting with your audience the priority, instead of obsessing about getting everything right.

Perfection is the enemy of authenticity. Resist!

● ●

SELF-REFLECTION
*Where do you resist being real and
connecting with your passion?*

● ●

33. MAKE YOUR AUDIENCE FEEL SPECIAL

My husband and I saw a lesser-known local band perform recently at a community event. He was intrigued and stopped by their table to buy their self-produced CD (with a hand-drawn cover) for $5.

As we were standing at the table buying the CD, the band's singer came over and introduced himself. He thanked us for buying his CD and engaged us in conversation. We learned a little more about them and had a nice chat.

The members of the band were high school and college students; they'd only been together for a little over a year. Yet they'd already learned one important thing about performing: You have to make the audience feel special.

Without an audience, a performer doesn't exist. The audience deserves our appreciation, our acknowledgement, our thanks.

Spend some time before your presentation talking with audience members. Instead of running off to your next appointment afterward, stick around and build some relationships.

My husband is going to be more inclined to seek out this band's performances, now that he has a personal connection, and he's already planning on buying their new CD when it comes out.

No matter how small a group, no matter how small a purchase, the connection you make with your audience members is infinitely valuable and critical to your growth and success as a speaker. Make sure they know it.

SELF-REFLECTION
How do you make your audience members feel special?

34. HOW IS A SPEAKER LIKE A CINNAMON ROLL CAKE?

As I stepped up to the counter of one of our favorite delis, the baker (a long-time friend) saw me and invited me into the kitchen to show me her fresh-from-the-oven cinnamon roll cake.

We chatted for a bit as she cut a slice and put it on a plate. She told me that she always cuts out a piece from a fresh cake before she puts it into the case, so the customers can see what's inside. It seems that customers are more likely to purchase a piece from an already-cut cake rather than a whole one. The interesting things one learns from trial and error in business!

It made me think (of course) of what we do as speakers. Audiences (our customers) also seem to prefer a speaker with a piece cut out in order to get a glimpse of our "insides."

When a speaker is too flawless, it's more difficult for the audience to relate to her and her message. But when a speaker shows some vulnerability, some imperfection, the audience realizes she's human, too. And if she can do it (whatever "it" may be), they can do it, too.

I'm very open about my struggles with anxiety and panic attacks, although it took me a long time to become comfortable enough to share my experience. But once I did (including writing an e-book about it), I found that not only did people relate to me more as a human being, but they realized that I could understand their anxiety in a way that not everyone else could.

In a world that idolizes flawless (Photoshopped) beauty and bodies, and with a social media culture that allows us to always display the most carefully curated photos and stories of our lives, it gets harder and harder to be comfortable sharing the real and the blemished.

. . . .

SELF-REFLECTION

*How do you show your audience that you
value connection over perfection?*

. . . .

5 FOCUS ON **SERVICE**

Have you ever justified not preparing or practicing for a speaking engagement by telling yourself, "It's only going to be a few people" or "None of the bigwigs will be there" or "I'm doing it for free?" In essence saying, "This is a B gig, and I'm bringing my B game."

Guess what: If you're a speaker (even a non-professional speaker), you're in the service business. And that means you must always make serving the audience your top priority.

You have an important message to share, but if you don't deliver your message in a way that your audience can receive it, you fail. And all the wonderful things you have to say will never make their destination.

It doesn't matter how big or small your audience is, or whether you're getting paid or not, or whether someone "important" is attending. You always have to bring your A game.

Why does it matter?

Every audience deserves your best. They are giving you their time and maybe their money to come hear you speak. They are hoping they are using their time wisely to gain some new, valuable insight. Don't disappoint them.

Every speaking engagement is a chance for you to improve your skills and confidence. Why waste this opportunity by throwing away your presentation?

You never know who your audience members will talk to. So no bigwigs are there, or there are only a few people. It's actually quite common for someone to be in the audience who can recommend you to bigger players. Do a half-ass job, though, and you can guarantee that no one in the audience will refer you or offer you another gig.

Always give your audience your best, no matter who it is. Bringing your B game will only bring you B engagements (whatever that means to you: non-paying, low-profile, low respect, etc.). Bringing your A game even to B engagements will earn you respect, for one, and consistently better gigs.

In this section, look for lessons for speakers using examples from a breakfast restaurant, Trader Joe's, and a Vitamix demo.

35. SERVE WITHOUT BEING ASKED

Shopping at Trader Joe's one day, my husband and I had two really great experiences with their staff that made me think about how we, as speakers, are serving our audiences.

First, we found ourselves in the bread section, eyeing the pretzel challah. Never seen pretzel challah? It's just what it sounds like: a loaf of challah with a soft pretzel crust. We like challah. And we like soft pretzels. So it seemed like a no-brainer.

Nearby, a Trader Joe's employee was loading up a bread shelf and saw us examining the loaf. She asked us if we had tried it and we said no. She said she hadn't tried it either.

"Do you want to try some?" she asked, and before we knew it, she had taken the bread into the back room, sliced it, and returned with samples. On the spot. We tried it. We loved it. We bought it.

Two things struck me about this interaction:

1. It was her idea to sample the bread. She didn't wait for us to ask. She engaged us in conversation.
2. She was flexible enough to stop the task she was working on and sample bread for us instead.

If that first experience wasn't enough to impress us, we struck up a conversation with another employee while we were nibbling on the challah.

We had wandered in front of a wine display. The wine on the stack was a blend we hadn't seen before, and we were curious about it. As we wondered aloud if it was any good, the employee shook his head and said, "You don't want this one...." and turned to the passing wine buyer to ask, "Am I right?" The wine buyer stopped, agreeing with the first opinion.

He said that, for this price point and this flavor profile, we could find several better wines in the store. And then he proceeded to tell me what they were, as I scrambled to save them in my phone. (Okay, I do wonder why they're even carrying that wine if there are other wines at the same price point and with a similar flavor profile that are better. But hey, I'm not the buyer.)

The first interaction made me think about how flexible we are with our audiences. Are you able to read and serve your audience on the spot, or are you so memorized and rehearsed that you can't go off script?

And I wondered how much speakers are anticipating their audiences' needs. For example, do you build their possible questions into your presentation so they don't have to ask – or do you give canned presentations to every audience, regardless of who they are and what interests they have?

The second interaction made me think about how honest and straightforward speakers are with audiences.

Are you so concerned with selling yourself or your product that you don't admit to mishaps or mistakes out of a need to close the sale? Do you try to shoehorn a fit with your services and product, even when there isn't one?

We owe our audiences honesty, flexibility, and proactiveness, and the willingness to serve them based on our best research (or at least anticipation) of their needs and wants.

We've been shopping at Trader Joe's for decades, so we don't need to be sold on their great products and customer service. But these interactions reinforced what we already knew, making us even more loyal customers.

Maybe your audience doesn't know you well, and this is your opportunity to demonstrate service for the first time. Maybe they already know you and this is your opportunity to remind them why they keep hiring you.

Either way, take the initiative. Don't wait for them to ask. Be prepared to give them what they need, want, and care about. You will delight the heck out of them!

SELF-REFLECTION
How do you define "service" in your presentations?

36. DOING THE BARE MINIMUM

I drove by a neighborhood breakfast place the other day and felt a sense of sadness. We had given this restaurant several chances, but every time we went there, the food and service were just mediocre. Nothing special. The same old thing that half a dozen restaurants within a half-mile were also doing.

I can't say it was terrible. It just wasn't good.

Hash browns were cooked in rancid oil. Eggs were greasy. "Wheat" toast was a shade of brown more indicative of caramel coloring than whole grains. Coffee was always lukewarm (and don't even get me started on the tea options). If I ordered a side of fruit, I knew the melon would be as hard as a rock. How is it possible to never ever find a ripe melon, even in melon season?

There are also some good breakfast places in town. The prices are the same, but that's the only similarity.

At our favorite spot, coffee comes from a local roaster known for their quality. The spinach in my scramble is fresh, not frozen. My toast is rustic and full of seeds. If I order a side of fruit, it will be seasonal and ripe. I'm happy to pay a little extra for real maple syrup instead of the fake high fructose stuff.

It's obvious that everyone who works there cares about doing their best.

How many speakers have you watched who were just getting by, doing the bare minimum?

They might read from a written script or directly from a PowerPoint, using a template you've seen 50 times before and nothing but bullets, slide after slide.

They might overload you with content (to prove how brilliant and knowledgeable they are), but make no effort to engage you or make the information relevant to your life or business.

They might be completely unprepared and stumbling through the talk, because they didn't bother to practice and it just didn't matter enough to them to deliver a quality presentation. They just wanted to get it over with.

On the other hand, you know a speaker has gone the extra mile when he's contacted audience members in advance for input and has incorporated the information into his slides.

You know a speaker has gone the extra mile when she notices your participation as an audience member, handing out buttons or candy to those who sit in the first row (something I've done) or giving a prize to the first person who answers a question.

You know a speaker has gone the extra mile when he strives to bring something new and fresh to the stage. One of my clients "peppers" the room with notes taped under chairs, for audience members to read at certain times. Another client made a particular point by superimposing his head onto a supermodel's body ("You can't just look at parts; you have to look at the big picture").

Some people don't commit to their work, and I don't suppose there's much I can do about that, except not patronize their businesses or refer anyone else to them.

If you're a speaker who doesn't take pride in your work, why bother? Why not find someone else to cover your topic who really cares about delivering value, committing the time and effort to practicing and preparing, and giving the audience their best?

• •

SELF-REFLECTION
Are you doing the bare minimum or are you giving it all you've got? How does someone benefit from being in your audience?

• •

37. PUBLIC SPEAKING TOUCHDOWN

While I'm not a football fan, I have caught a game here and there. On a Sunday afternoon, I was drinking a Boddingtons ale and munching on fries at a local restaurant when I started to pay attention to a few of the weekend game highlights showing on TV.

I noticed that, when the player with the ball runs for the end zone, he runs as fast as he can, even if no one is chasing him. You might have noticed this in other sports as well. Why run as fast as you can, even if you know you won't be caught?

Because you're giving it all you've got, or in sports terminology, "leaving it all on the field."

When you run like that, you're committed. You're motivated. You're willing to do whatever it takes.

It's a quality the most successful elite athletes demonstrate every time you see them compete. There is no half effort. The commitment is full-on from the minute the clock starts.

This means that, even if you're tired from a long drive or air travel, you maintain your energy. This means that, even if you're experiencing distractions at home, you remain focused on the job at hand. This means that, even when things take an unexpected turn (an audience member disagrees with you, you accidentally leave out a huge chunk of content, your projector bulb burns out), you stay present with the audience and you finish what you've started.

• •

SELF-REFLECTION

Do you walk away from every speaking engagement knowing you made the full commitment and left it all on the stage?

• •

38. BE WILLING TO THROW AWAY YOUR SPEECH

Several years ago, I attended and presented at the Professional Women's Association conference at the University of California, Santa Barbara. The opening keynote was given by Chancellor Henry T. Yang.

He spoke about recent challenges he'd faced at work, some of his daily activities, and how much he would have enjoyed joining us for our day of seminars and inspirational speakers. He seemed a little disorganized, and I was having some trouble following his train of thought.

Then he revealed that he had written a speech (which he showed, rolled up in his hand), but decided not to give it!

He told us that, when he walked in and saw so many familiar faces, he felt that he knew everyone in the room and wanted to speak from the heart and share some things about his day rather than read his speech. It was a very touching admission and one that I believe endeared him to the audience.

He then went on to invite every one of us to email him; if he gets 100 emails a day, he said, what's 10 more? He reads and responds to all of his messages before he goes to bed, so he can sleep well.

If the audience didn't already adore him, that part certainly sealed the deal.

Now, in a topical presentation where your audience is there to learn something specific, this may not be the best route to take. You want to give your audience the information they're expecting and hoping for.

But it's always a possibility that your direction and your audience's wishes won't mesh. In that case, it's okay to throw out all or some of what you had planned. If your audience wants 50 minutes of Q&A, well, why not give it to them? If the information you're presenting isn't relevant to them, ask them what IS relevant.

Always speak from a place of genuine interest, intuition, and service.

After hearing Chancellor Yang speak, I felt that I really could send him an email and he would respond. Or that I could sit down next to him and have an engaging conversation. His approachability and humanness felt like a much greater gift than if he had spoken about "the state of professional women at UCSB" or some such topic.

CEOs and other high-level executives often cultivate an atmosphere of inaccessible aloofness, both in the workplace and as speakers. But if you really want to sell your ideas and persuade your audience to "do" something after your presentation, aloofness will be your downfall.

It might feel risky to open yourself up; speakers feel vulnerable enough as it is. But it's a risk worth taking to create an atmosphere where your audience feels like you're giving them exactly what they need, want, and care about.

SELF-REFLECTION
*Are you giving the audience what they need, want,
and care about or what you need, want, and care about?
How can you create a balance?*

39. SIX CUSTOMER SERVICE TIPS FOR SPEAKERS

While reading my husband's company newsletter one holiday season, I came across some excellent retail customer service tips, which I decided to adapt for speakers. Speakers are in customer service, and I think we often forget this!

When you're preparing to meet your customers – your host, your organizer, your event planner, and your audience – keep in mind that they're you're customers. How can you serve them at the highest level?

1. Treat the customer as the most important part of your job – not an interruption of it.

How many times have you found yourself annoyed by a difficult, challenging, or off-topic audience question? How many times have you secretly wished that people would follow your game plan as you've envisioned it and stop interrupting with their comments that don't advance your point?

Those of us who take the stage well-prepared and well-organized can sometimes be thrown off when the audience doesn't play along as expected. Those of us who throw presentations together at the last minute will be even more flustered. Realize that each member of the audience lives in and makes her own reality and that your perfect little presentation may not jive with this person's perceptions and understanding.

Understand that people come from all walks of life and have all kinds of knowledge and life experience that they will bring to your presentation. Do your best to create a new world for each audience, but know that individuals will act based on their own worlds. Expect it, go with it, be ready for it.

2. Make sure your stress doesn't translate over the phone (or by email or on the stage).

You may be under a lot of stress, because, heck, preparing for a speaking engagement and giving a presentation can be stressful. You may not have gotten enough sleep; you may have just driven two hours in traffic; your baby might be sick and your spouse is not helping. But don't blab about it or take it out on your host, your organizer, or your audience. They don't care, and all you will accomplish is ruining your chances of being asked back. You're there for them. You serve them. Period.

3. Make sure to acknowledge if the customer has waited for an extended period of time and apologize for the wait.

Stuff happens. Air conditioning goes haywire. Cars break down. A/V staff forgets to set up the equipment you need. If your audience is inconvenienced by being made to wait, by being put in an uncomfortable situation, by not receiving their morning coffee, acknowledge the problem and then move on.

Don't dwell on it, don't be overly solicitous or apologetic, and don't beat yourself up. Let the audience know that you care about their comfort and their time, sincerely apologize, and then get on with your planned event.

4. Help take on some of the burden.

You may not be the one stressed out, but you may be working with an event planner who is falling apart. Instead of feeding off the crazy, offer to help. Be the speaker everyone enjoys working with. Make yourself part of the team instead of the prima donna who waltzes in, does her thing in isolation, and then takes off without a thank-you or a handshake.

5. Always suggest a different item if we don't carry something a customer wants.

Find a way to meet your audience's needs, even if you don't have all the answers. Don't be afraid to refer your contacts to resources outside your area of expertise. I'm not a voice expert, so when people have questions about voice training or voice care that are outside my narrow scope of knowledge, I'm happy to refer them to professionals who are experts.

You can't be everything to all people, so don't drive yourself crazy trying or feel like a failure because you can't answer every single question. Be a giver, not a hoarder. Share your information and resources freely and you will be appreciated and rewarded for your generosity.

6. Have a good time while you work.

If you're not having a good time, how can you expect your audience to have a good time? And if you think it's wrong to have a good time during a business presentation, you might need an attitude adjustment. (I hope you've read the chapter on fun.)

Think of the most memorable and successful presentations you've attended, the ones where you got the most value and impact. What engaged you? What kept your attention? What helped you learn and retain the most information? I bet it wasn't a boring speaker who droned on in a monotone with slides so densely packed you couldn't read them. Enough said.

While you're out and about in the world, doing your daily errands, take a look at the most successful examples of good customer service and think about how you can apply them to your speaking engagements.

SELF-REFLECTION

How could you be serving your audience to the best of your ability?

• •

40. FIVE THINGS SPEAKERS CAN LEARN FROM EVENT PLANNERS

I have two clients who are event planners. They create amazing social and corporate events as well as weddings that would charm your socks off.

If you've ever been to a conference, a wedding, a large fundraiser, a political rally, or a memorial service, chances are an event planner was involved.

All good event planners have one thing in common: No matter how complicated or difficult the planning and organization, they make the event appear seamless. With vendors ranging from caterers to florists to photographers to musicians to hotels to audio/visual professionals, and every other kind of service provider you can imagine, the event planner juggles personalities, schedules, budgets, and activities to create an event that seems like it "just came together."

As speakers, there's a lot we can learn from event planners. Here are some event planning tips to help you put together your next seamless presentation.

1. Understand the purpose of the event.

Event planners have to understand what their client's purpose is for the event in order to be successful. Is it to raise money, thank donors, build morale, celebrate an important occasion, educate staff, experience their dream wedding, or create industry cohesion? What are the desired outcomes or results?

As a speaker, understanding your client's desired result will help you create a presentation that truly meets the needs of your audience and guarantees that you are focusing on the proper objectives when preparing.

2. Make the best use of the venue.

Event planners frequently get to choose their own venue, while speakers are mostly expected to go where the client tells us to go. However, once you know the venue, there are still a lot of things to consider, and event planners are masters at making any venue workable.

How big is the room? If it's too big, how can you make it more intimate? If it's too small, how can you make it feel more roomy? How's the lighting, the temperature, the seating? Are there enough electrical outlets for your equipment? How far away is parking, and do you have to lug your supplies a long way? (There's one venue at UC Santa Barbara where I've spoken many times that requires a walk from one end of campus to the other. A rolling case makes this trek much more bearable.)

3. Give yourself plenty of time to prepare.

An event planner generally does not throw together a wedding in a month. There are vendors to coordinate, invitations to be sent, a site to secure. It would be ridiculous to expect a well-organized event with such a short lead time, unless it's very small, with very few attendees and minimal supplies and equipment needed.

Likewise, it would be foolish to start preparing your presentation a few days before you deliver it, yet this is quite common. Have you taken the time to determine your objective, prepare a strong opening and closing, and practice the presentation? Have you gotten input from the organizers or attendees about their needs and interests? Have you rehearsed any demonstrations, games, examples, or activities? Have you checked to make sure you have extra batteries, an extension cord, enough handouts, a backup copy of your PowerPoint, and a timer?

Preparing to give an effective, engaging, and memorable presentation takes time. There's no way around it. Give yourself as much time as you need so you can give the audience your best.

4. Be flexible.

"Stuff" happens. Event planners are experts at working around setbacks and figuring out solutions when things don't go as planned. They don't panic; they just get busy.

As a speaker, if you have not yet experienced a setback, it's only a matter of time before you do. Your technology will fail. Your room will be next to a loud construction site. The speaker before you will go long, and your presentation will be cut by fifteen minutes. The trick is to keep going. Sometimes your audience will know there's a problem, but most of the time, you will be the only one. Keep it to yourself, fix it as quickly and quietly as possible, and move on.

At some point, after all the planning and preparation, you have to let go and accept that whatever happens, happens!

5. Enjoy yourself.

Event planners don't get to relax until their event is over; even after all the planning is done, event supervision and management is the last step in the process. But it's important that she's not too stressed out to enjoy the fruits of her labor during this last push. After all, she still has to run the show, interacting with clients, vendors, and guests – and if she's not enjoying herself, her bad mood can easily rub off on others.

Likewise, a speaker is no good to himself or the audience if he isn't having a good time. Before, during, and after your presentation, you are interacting with your client and your audience, and you are still working until you get in your car to leave. It's not only your job to convey information, but to ensure your guests are enjoying themselves.

Provide full service to your audience, just like the successful event planner.

••

SELF-REFLECTION
As a speaker, how do you take care of your guests?

••

41. WHAT A VITAMIX DEMO CAN TEACH YOU ABOUT PUBLIC SPEAKING

One fateful Saturday, I paid a visit to my local Costco. I walked in for a package of kitchen sponges and walked out with a Vitamix.

Okay, it wasn't really that simple. I had been eyeing the Vitamix for years, and I knew that Costco regularly held "road shows" for the blender. After the previous one, which I didn't have time to watch, I had called to find out when they would be in town again and made a point of showing up at Costco to watch the demo.

If you don't know the Vitamix, it's a super-powerful blender with a 2-horsepower motor. It blends, but it also has enough power to heat your ingredients into a soup or hot beverage, and it also can freeze your ingredients solid into ice cream or sorbet. It absolutely pulverizes nuts, grains, vegetables, and fruits so that your smoothie is completely liquefied. And I've wanted one forever. But first, I wanted to see the demo.

I was obviously impressed enough with the demo to finally buy my Vitamix; however, from a public speaking perspective, I was also impressed.

1. The demo was relevant and effective.

If you're going to spend a lot of money on a product or service, it helps to see it in action. Testimonials are nice, but, ultimately, does the product do what its marketing materials say it does?

Drew, the demonstrator, showed all the relevant aspects of the Vitamix's features. He made hot tortilla soup, he made fruit sorbet, he made pistachio ice cream, he made smoothies with whole apples and lots of spinach. He used recipes that both looked and tasted good to a general audience and seemed easy to make. And, on top of that, he used vegetable broth in the soup and soy milk in the smoothie, so even vegans and vegetarians (like me and my husband, who are clearly a target market), could taste all the samples. Well done.

How can you demo your product or service more effectively during a presentation?

2. The demonstrator was flexible as the audience ebbed and flowed.

In a demo setting in the middle of Costco, your audience doesn't stay static. They are passing by on their way from the seafood to the socks, and they may or may not stop (although free food samples are always a big draw). There is no beginning, middle, or end, except when the demonstrator finishes one recipe and starts another.

Drew effortlessly incorporated audience questions as he performed his demo. There was no waiting till the end, and he answered questions comfortably as he continued to explain each recipe he was making and the features of the blender.

At one point, we mentioned that we had missed out on the ice cream demo, so he offered to make another one. It was easy for him to choose which recipe to make on the spot, based on which audience members had just arrived and which ones had already had samples. He was paying attention the whole time.

How flexible are you about tweaking your presentation based on who's in the room and what they're interested in?

3. He knew his subject inside and out.

Drew bought his first Vitamix when he was 17. Now 24 years old, he both talked about and demonstrated the machine like an old pro. He stood with the back of the machine to him so the audience could see it from the front. He flipped switches and turned dials, barely looking at the machine, so he could maintain eye contact with his audience. He's made these recipes so many times and talked about the Vitamix so many times and – here's the key – actually been USING the blender for so long that he knows everything there is to know about it.

How well do you know your topic? How up-to-date are you on new developments and research?

4. He captivated the audience.

I would be curious to know how long an average audience member watches one of these demos and how long on average a person stands there before they decide to buy. I think we were there for probably ten minutes, and there were several others in the crowd who were there as long as or longer than we were. Drew was able to take our attention away from the pool equipment, the giant bags of coffee, the towering piles of peaches, the shiny bikes, and the añejo tequila long enough to convince us to buy.

And when I say "us," I don't just mean me and my husband. We watched several people pick up Vitamixes during the demo, including a postal worker on duty who needed to come back and get it after his shift. You might wonder if any of these people were plants, and believe me, I did. But the conversations we were having with others in the group were pretty sincere (and I recognized at least one purchasing couple as locals who talked about how they never use their juicer anymore because it's such a mess to clean). I wasn't just standing there for free samples; I was fascinated by how this machine works, its vast repertoire of recipes, its powerful motor, its easy cleanup, and, yes, its potentially positive effect on my health if I can manage to get more veggies and fruits into my diet. The demo was credible and persuasive, and that's why people stood there for so long, watching.

How well do you keep your audience's attention and keep them from wandering to their email and Facebook?

5. He never once sounded like a commercial.

Drew was there to sell Vitamixes. There's no question; that is his job. Yet, he obviously enjoys the product and his work so much that his demo never felt pushy or demanding. He was personable, light, had a good sense of humor, and his explanation of features or answers to questions flowed smoothly and organically. He was clearly having a good time.

We watched him prepare recipes, clean the blender, and start over several times. He demonstrated how the casing is sealed and nothing can get inside. He showed us the dull blades and the "tamper" that doesn't touch them when you push down your ingredients inside the container. And all of this while having a casual conversation and making smoothie and soup samples.

Do you sound like a commercial when talking about your product or service? Does your audience want to change the channel?

As presentations go, this was a highly effective and interesting one. Next time you have the opportunity to watch a product demo, take a few minutes to see what you can learn from a speaking (and marketing) pro!

• •

SELF-REFLECTION

How can you "sell" your ideas while still serving the audience?

• •

6 DELIVER AN EXPERIENCE

I pick up so many excellent speaking tips from comedians. They are required to deliver a complete experience for their audiences, a challenge that hinges on keeping them laughing every few moments.

I believe that speakers are also required to create and deliver a complete experience. It's not just the content. It's not just the delivery. It's not just your opening or your closing or your particular style or personality. The experience is a complete package that starts from before you even walk into the room (your marketing, your outreach) until the audience leaves, and even afterward if they stay connected with you.

On the TV special "Talking Funny," host Ricky Gervais facilitated a conversation between fellow comedians Jerry Seinfeld, Louis C.K., and Chris Rock.

During the conversation, Gervais talked about the responsibility he feels in performing. People pay money to come to the show, find a babysitter, drive around to find parking . . . it's a major commitment for the audience.

He says, "I better have something special to say. I don't think it's just enough to do 60 minutes of them laughing, because they can't take that with them. Whereas if you say something that's interesting or resonates, or that's different, they can take it with them . . . It's the gift that keeps on giving."

For Ricky Gervais, it's not enough to entertain the audience. He'll even cut a bit from his show if it's too easy or gets a "cheap laugh." He wants the audience to know he's worked hard on a bit and that it wasn't just a throwaway joke. He wants to feel proud of his work.

Most performers might be ecstatic to get an easy laugh or to draw a standing ovation for very little work. For Gervais, there has to be a deeper connection with the audience; he wants to send them home with something so memorable and unique, they'll still be thinking about it 20 years later.

How many of us put this kind of thought and care into our presentations?

How many of us think about what our audience is giving up (money, time, deadlines) to hear us speak?

How many of us actually make the effort to give our audience a "gift that keeps on giving?"

Can you imagine how rewarding it would be to know that you've given the audience something so valuable and profound that years later they're still responding to your message? (I've had this experience a few times, and I don't have to imagine it – it felt like a huge honor.)

Maybe this isn't realistic on an everyday basis, when the boss pops his head in the door of your office and says, "Hey, Sam, can you give a report at the staff meeting in 15 minutes?"

But what if we were to keep this idea in the front of our minds, striving as often as possible to create an experience for the audience, not just to give a presentation?

In this section, look for lessons for speakers using examples from a dinner party, a patisserie, and a surf guitar icon.

42. THEY EITHER LIKE IT OR THEY DON'T

On an episode of "Top Chef," the contestants were tasked to cook over a campfire for desert ranchers. One of the chefs shared this opinion:

"I don't necessarily think I should change the way I cook for the people I'm cooking for.... When a guest comes into your restaurant, you don't create a menu based on where they come from. You cook your food, and they either like it or they don't."

And sure, this is true. The way he cooks is his personal style. He shouldn't change that for anyone, because that's what makes him unique. His restaurant will sink or swim based on how many people like what he's offering and are willing to pay for it.

However, these cowboys weren't coming to his restaurant. This challenge was like a catered event where the chef was indeed working for the people he's cooking for. He may not need to change his cooking style, but he does need to change his attitude.

After all, this is a competition. The judges want to know who can best execute the spirit of the challenge: cooking over open campfires in the desert for ranchers who work hard all day. Does the food taste good and also suit the needs of the ranchers?

The show wouldn't devise such challenges if the chefs were going to be allowed to cook whatever they wanted in every challenge, with the perfect ingredients and the comforts of their home kitchens. They do that every day in their own restaurants.

The judges are asking the contestants to open their minds, stretch their imaginations and abilities, and push themselves beyond what is comfortable. If they can achieve this and still make good food, they will succeed on the show.

Speakers face the same challenges, although not artificially created by a judging panel like on "Top Chef." We face audiences who have an expectation that we will match our offering to their requirements, that we will create an experience that benefits and engages them. We need to express ourselves in our own unique way while delivering the audience's desired outcomes.

The more we stretch, the more we explore what makes our presentations successful with different audiences, the more success we will achieve.

• •

SELF-REFLECTION
How have you balanced your own style with the audience's expectations in order to create a better experience?

• •

43. MAKE YOUR AUDIENCE FEEL LIKE ROCK STARS

Have you ever gone to a rock or pop concert or watched one on TV?

Have you noticed that, at many or most concerts (I don't have a statistic so let's just say many), the band holds the microphone out to the audience at some point for them to sing? The audience members are already singing, of course. It's one place where you can sing at the top of your lungs and still no one hears you!

But when the singer points that microphone at the audience, the volume goes up to 11, and even if half of those 1,000 audience members are singing off-key, you'd never know it. It's a gift the singer gives the audience, and everyone participates. Why?

- Audience members want to be part of the experience.

- Audience members want to bond with the performer.

- Audience members want to bond with each other.

As a speaker, you have plenty of opportunities, should you choose to use them, to give the audience their moment. It's a simple thing but yields big results. You're not a rock star, and you're not going to invite the audience to sing (or maybe you are …), so how do you incorporate the audience into the experience?

- Ask questions that let audience members share their own experiences as they relate to your topic.

- Have audience members converse with each other in pairs or small groups to discuss issues and get to know each other.

- Provide activities and exercises that allow the audience to apply their knowledge to a problem and solve it.

- Offer unstructured time during breaks or lunch where your participants can chat freely without having to do any "work."

Everyone has a lifetime of knowledge and experience that can enrich your presentation. Audience members want to share, they want to be heard, they want to participate, and they often want to learn from each other as well as from the speaker.

Are you going to waste that awesome opportunity to create an awesome experience by pretending you're the only one who has something of value to say?

Invite your audience to "sing." Bring them into the experience. Make them feel like rock stars.

SELF-REFLECTION
How have you brought your audiences into the experience?
How can you do it in the future?

• •

44. WHAT KIND OF SANDWICH ARE YOU SERVING?

There was a time when there were very few options for vegetarians on restaurant menus. Typically, we were offered steamed vegetables and brown rice, no matter how epicurean the restaurant. Or, if we were lucky, there was a Gardenburger. I don't know why people think that vegetarians require dishes with no complexity, fat, flavor, or seasoning.

These days (27 years after I first became a vegetarian), things are much better for us when my husband and I eat out, and we can usually find several options that are on par with the restaurant's other creative offerings.

But there's still one holdout from the old days: the veggie sandwich.

If there's a veggie sandwich on the menu, I can totally predict what's inside. Layered on top of the mayo or mustard is a mile-high stack of cheddar or provolone cheese. Lettuce. Tomato. Cucumber. Sprouts. Occasionally, avocado! And when they're feeling really adventurous, a piece of roasted red pepper. Basically, put every bland and watery vegetable between two piece of bread, and that's your veggie sandwich.

Luckily for us, there are a couple of places in town that know how to do an original and flavorful veggie sandwich. One place offers the "hot mushroom combo," a combination of three kinds of sautéed mushrooms and caramelized onions over brie and Dijon mustard.

Another sandwich shop offers nine vegetarian sandwiches, including one with Kalamata olive tapenade, fresh mozzarella, greens, roasted red peppers, and basil leaves.

And another, a French bistro, offers a grilled sandwich of Emmental cheese with roasted shallots and sun-dried tomatoes.

Believe it or not, some places are even making veggie sandwiches **without** cheese!

You're wondering: what's my point?

Just because I'm a vegetarian, that doesn't mean I want the same old veggie sandwich every sandwich shop has been slapping together since the '70s.

Not all vegetarians are alike, just like not all meat-eaters are alike. Make an effort to know me, what I like, what I want, and where I'm coming from.

Some speakers assume they know their audience because the audience is all women. Or all youth. Or all entrepreneurs. Or all scientists. Or all southerners. And of course, there are always similarities in groups. There's a reason we group ourselves together as humans; we seek out people who are similar to us, have similar backgrounds, interests, life experiences, and goals.

But audiences are made up of individuals. And many of them are tired of the same old dish they always get served. This guy likes mustard and that woman likes horseradish. Someone else is begging for sriracha!

Your audience notices when you haven't taken the time to think about them as individuals. They're not all the same and they don't all expect the same results or outcomes. So do it right. Make the effort. You'll be rewarded with repeat business. Just like the sandwich shop that makes outstanding vegetarian sandwiches!

• •

SELF-REFLECTION

*How do you create an engaging experience, remembering that
your audience is made up of individuals?*

• •

45. DO YOU KNOW WHAT YOU'RE SAYING – AND WHY?

Does anyone know what a laundry list is? Me neither. I think I saw one in a museum exhibit last year, but I'm not sure.

I believe it's a list of all the possible items that a launderer would take, and you would check off which items you were leaving to be cleaned. This is one of those expressions that makes no sense to me, like so many others.

I learned my lesson about saying what I mean and meaning what I say when I was about eight years old. Some family friends left our house after a visit and I – merely repeating an expression I had heard many times in movies or TV – said, "Goodbye and good riddance."

Let's just say there were consequences for my rudeness.

Using words accurately and appropriately is important to me. Just about the worst thing a speaker can do is be unclear, because at minimum you need to be understood, especially if you care about creating a complete experience.

Imagine speaking to an audience outside the U.S. and using the expression "laundry list." Would anyone understand you? Probably not. How about using a football analogy?

Now ask yourself whether your audiences who **are** in the United States understand you. Does everyone get sports analogies? Maybe not – so why use them if you can't be sure?

There are a lot of idioms we use in our daily language that are pretty clear as to their meanings, if you think about it for a moment: "putting the cart before the horse," "walking on eggshells," "like a fish out of water."

You might even be able to translate those abroad, but I wouldn't try it without consulting someone who is a native speaker of the language to find out if there's an equivalent expression.

As you consider your language, keep these points in mind:

Meanings are not always obvious.

But what about those that aren't clear? Talking about someone who's "hoist by his own petard" is great if everyone in the audience is familiar with Shakespeare or medieval weapons, but otherwise, the meaning is far from obvious.

How about "close but no cigar" or "down to brass tacks?" Sure, your audience can go look these up after your presentation, but in the meantime, they're thinking "What the heck does that mean, anyway?"

Okay, I'm being a little facetious. Most people will have heard these expressions before and if not totally clear on the literal meaning, will get your point. But then, I said "most."

It's all relative.

One Christmas, I gave one of my nieces a cute button that was a pictogram for "clothes horse." It had a picture of clothing and a picture of a horse. Pretty straightforward. Except that she had never heard the expression (at the time, she was only 13). Out of the nearly 20 people in the room, in fact, only two people knew what it meant.

So I tried to explain the expression to them, but I realized I had no idea what its origin was. All I could tell them was how it's used now. They kept asking, "But what does a horse have to do with it?" And I had no idea.

So back to my main point: Be clear. Don't use expressions that you don't understand yourself. Be extra cautious and assume the audience may not get your favorite idioms, especially in our multicultural world of today.

· ·

SELF-REFLECTION
Have you ever confused your audience with an expression or idiom that only made sense to you?

· ·

46. ARE YOU SPEAKING YOUR AUDIENCE'S LANGUAGE?

My husband and I stopped by a new patisserie in our neighborhood last week. Very exciting – beautiful French pastries made from scratch right there in the bakery.

As we were waiting to pay for our treats, an elderly man stood in front of the case perusing the pastries. The woman behind the counter asked if she could help him.

He asked, "What's the one with the glaze on it?"

She said, "The chou?"

He looked at her with confusion.

"This one, the round one with the glaze."

She said, "The caramel glazed chou."

Now, if you don't know French pastry terms, "chou" (plural "choux") is the type of dough used to make a small, round light pastry, often with a cream filling – a profiterole or cream puff.

If you don't know French pastry terms, someone just asked you if you'd like the "shoe."

How much more helpful would it have been for her to say, "The one with the glaze is a caramel glazed cream puff – it's called a chou pastry"?

In the book *Made to Stick*, Chip and Dan Heath talk about the "Curse of Knowledge:" When we know something, it's hard to imagine what it's like **not** to know it.

Then we assume others know what we know, especially when we use words or jargon they've never heard, and we get frustrated when they don't get what we're talking about.

You can still educate your audience about your terminology or expressions, or use words they don't know, but you can also do it without making them feel stupid.

If you're going to use industry jargon or lingo, always explain yourself.

Better yet, don't use it at all.

Now please excuse me while I go eat a shoe.

• •

SELF-REFLECTION

Is there particular jargon or industry lingo that you use in your presentations that you should be translating into plain English?

• •

47. PLAY FOR THE PEOPLE

Dick Dale – the King of the Surf Guitar – played a small concert here in Santa Barbara a few years ago, and as a big fan of surf music, I was thrilled to attend.

At the time of the concert, Dale was 70 and could rock the house like a guy in his 20s. In addition to playing guitar, he sings, plays drums, plays drums on the bass guitar strings, and also plays a Louis Armstrong-inspired trumpet. And those are just the instruments he chose for this particular show – his website lists a total of 17 instruments that he has mastered.

His young son Jimmy accompanied him onstage, matching him note for note on his matching gold Fender Stratocaster and also played some mean drums.

Dale is a complete entertainer, holding nothing back, and many elements of his performance translate over to public speaking.

Put the audience first.

Dale is all about the audience. He mentioned that he doesn't have a set list, which is unconventional in a live show. Some fans come to consecutive shows, he said, and he never wants to play the same songs in the same order (or in the same style) that he played them the night before.

He also addressed some young guitar players in the front row when he said, "Play for the people," not to impress other musicians. "When the people like what you play, it means you're giving your heart to them."

He closed the show by introducing and thanking his band members and then turning to the audience and saying, "And most of all, you!"

Incorporate audience interaction.

Twice during the evening, Dale encouraged the audience to sing along – which we did. Throughout the show, he spoke directly to individuals in the audience, some of them his hardcore fans, also known as "Dick Heads."

He paid special attention to the young musicians in the front row, repeatedly giving them advice about musicianship and life.

Let your body do the talking.

When a musician of mostly instrumental and quite complex music has his hands full with a guitar, and is also directing his band, how exactly does he communicate to the audience? With the rest of his body!

Dale's expressive face and physical movements were as effective as though he were explaining his music in words. As he played, he managed to use his hands and body to communicate to his band members, encourage his son to take center stage, point out friends in the audience, and also move expressively to the music like a surfer on a wave.

You are the host; the audience members are your guests.

At the conclusion of the show, Dale went right to signing autographs. My husband and I and other audience members went ahead to the reception.

When Dale arrived at the reception, he greeted everyone as though we were honored guests. As he entered the room, he made eye contact with me and my husband, immediately walking over to shake our hands and ask how we liked the show. We got a few minutes to speak to him before other guests beckoned, and then he was off chatting and posing for pictures with strangers.

Under-promise and over-deliver.

Tom Peters said it first and it's been repeated many times in marketing books, blogs, and speeches. I knew very little about Dick Dale before I walked into the concert. I'm a fan of traditional surf guitar, and knowing that Dick Dale was one of its pioneers, I knew I'd have a good time.

But I had no idea just how much fun this show would be. I can't say anyone under-promised. But they certainly over-delivered. There was one surprise after another. Each song brought out new talents of the musicians. Each piece was more complex than the last. I never could have imagined how unique and special this show would turn out to be.

· ·

SELF-REFLECTION
What more could you give your audience?

· ·

48. HOW IS SPEAKING LIKE A DINNER PARTY?

"Entertaining is about creating suitable and inviting occasions. It's about bringing people together . . . But most of all . . . it is about the guests and not about you.
— Mireille Guiliano, *French Women for All Seasons* —

Substitute "speaking" for "entertaining" and Mireille has just described the most positive aspects of being a speaker. In fact, speaking and hosting guests are very similar:

- You want your guests/audience to enjoy themselves.

- You want to connect with your guests/audience as individuals.

- You want your guests/audience to feel cared for.

- You want to give your guests/audience a memorable experience.

- You want your guests/audience to feel nourished and satisfied.

- The more you prepare in advance, the fewer mishaps occur.

The main difference between the two situations is that you probably shouldn't have a cocktail while waiting for your audience to arrive . . .

Think of your audience as your guests. Ask yourself how you can take care of their needs and comfort to the best of your ability. Give them an experience they'll remember forever. And always plan your presentation so your audience leaves feeling satisfied but wanting more!

SELF-REFLECTION

How could you treat your audience members as special guests the way you treat guests in your home?

7 STAND OUT

"I wasn't going to let nerves get in my way. I wasn't going to let fear get in my way. I knew how lucky I was. And I just was going to let every moment be about joy and gratitude."
— Anne Hathaway on hosting the Oscars —

Not many of us get the opportunity to stand in front of millions of people and promote ourselves and our businesses, which is what an actor or comedian gets to do when hosting the Oscars.

Of course, it's a privilege to host an awards show like the Oscars. But it's also a privilege to get to speak in front of any audience!

I realize that some of you are reading this and thinking, "**Get** to speak?" You might see speaking as more of a "**have**" to do. (We'll talk more about this in the mindset section.)

But the opportunity to stand out is not one to be taken lightly. Just by showing up, you are doing something that the majority of people will never have the opportunity to do.

In a sea of sameness, speakers who stand out may demonstrate a number of skills and characteristics:

- They're funny.

- They've engaged audience emotions in a different way.

- They have a unique look.

- They have a unique presentation style.

- They have a unique personality.

- They bring unusual or fun props and visuals.

- They bring games or music or something unexpected.

- They enjoy themselves.

- They express their message in a new way.

- They're not afraid to rock the boat.

Sure, standing out can be intimidating and scary! But what have you got to lose? You can either stand out or blend in. Which is going to move you forward?

In this section, look for lessons for speakers using examples from a cheese plate, a Katharine Hepburn movie, and my allergy doctor!

49. MEET MY ALLERGY DOCTOR

My doctor is always thinking about how to put his patients first, and I bet he doesn't even know how this makes him stand out in the health care world.

When I met with him about changing my allergy medication, he suggested one that might work better for me and told me where I could buy the generic version for the lowest price in town.

He referred me to another doctor and gave me the inside scoop on how I could get an appointment right away and not have to wait a month.

He clarified incorrect information a pharmacist had given me with clear and understandable language.

He wasn't promoting himself, his medical group, or a pharmaceutical company.

In this brief appointment, my doctor gave me more value than many businesspeople I work with, and many speakers:

- He wasn't in a hurry to tell me what he wanted to tell me.
- He listened to my needs and gave suggestions accordingly.
- He freely and generously shared resources that I wouldn't have known about otherwise.

This is plain-old good customer service, but it's something that always stands out. It doesn't matter if you're a doctor, speaker, sales clerk, bank teller, software engineer, marketing guru, life coach, artist, manufacturer, or server: This is the minimum you should be providing your audience or client.

- Do you give your audiences and clients useful resources, even if they might come from a rival company that provides something you don't?
- Do you listen to what your audiences need and want before determining what to deliver?

🐟 Do you take time to clarify and illustrate your points, rather than rushing through your presentations?

🐟 Do you give clear value to your audiences before you ever consider selling them anything?

There are a lot of other allergy doctors that I could go to, but why would I? And there are a lot of other speakers out there delivering a similar topic to yours.

Why should you be chosen over other speakers? How do you stand out?

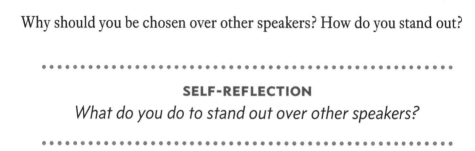

SELF-REFLECTION
What do you do to stand out over other speakers?

50. WHAT'S ON YOUR CHEESE PLATE?

My husband and I were excited to see a cheese plate listed on a new restaurant menu a few years ago. My husband was a cheesemonger for many years, and we are cheese fanatics.

I asked the host what was on the cheese plate. She didn't know, so she asked the person who appeared to be the chef. He said, "A blue, a brie, maybe a cheddar..."

A blue, a brie, maybe a cheddar?

Here were my expectations: I expected them to know what cheeses were on that plate and, even more, what kind of blue, brie, cheddar, and whatever else was on that plate.

It makes a difference to me whether the blue is a St. Agur, a Cashel Blue, or a Maytag. It makes a difference to me whether the cheddar is from Grafton or Montgomery's.

I got the distinct impression that this restaurant wasn't the least big interested in standing out or being unique. It's possible that the cheese plate was loaded with outstanding choices, but how many people would I have to ask to find out? Because they gave the appearance of being generic, I didn't dig any deeper and I didn't eat there.

In contrast, I remember going to a training in Los Angeles and staying at a big chain hotel. During the lunch break, I joined some of my colleagues for lunch in the hotel restaurant. I kind of expected the generic hotel chain menu, but I had a pleasant surprise!

There was a cheese plate! When I asked the server about it, she didn't know what was on the plate, so she went to ask. Then the chef appeared, and not only did he know exactly what was on the plate, but the cheeses he listed were unique and special. Not a generic cheese among them.

I will forever recommend this restaurant and look forward to eating there again.

The other restaurant – I never ate there and it closed within a matter of months.

You may have content, message, and style that stand out from other speakers, **but can you articulate that?**

Even if your topic is generic and your style is pedestrian, you still need to be able to describe what makes you special, what your audience receives that's different, and how you bring value that others don't.

SELF-REFLECTION
*Are you able to articulate what makes you special?
How would you describe what sets you apart?*

51. DON'T MISS A CHANCE TO BE MEMORABLE

While attending the World Tea Expo one year, I sat in on the competition to create the best tea-containing cocktail.

The 13 contestants, finalists chosen through online voting, prepared their drinks live onstage. One of the main rules of the competition was, "Recipes must be applicable in the marketplace, meaning recipes must be able to be realistically prepared and served in a foodservice establishment (tea room, restaurant, bar, etc.)."

The contestants had two minutes to prepare their drinks and then were interviewed about their concoctions before the final judging. Out of 13 contestants, only one was prepared to talk about her drink as it applied to the marketplace.

I found this rather shocking, as this competition was about showcasing not only a special drink but promoting the contestants' businesses! Every contestant represented either a tea company or a retailer. Either way, the winner ends up with features in *Food and Beverage Magazine* and *Imbibe* magazine, as well as being published in an upcoming book. It was the perfect opportunity to pitch the drink and their product and describe how it would fit into a tea room, restaurant, or bar.

When the Hale Tea Company contestant started talking about her drink, the audience sat up and paid attention. She had a convincing pitch about her cocktail and its marketability that wowed the crowd.

Unfortunately, she didn't win, but I guarantee that the audience members (many of whom are her target market) remembered her product, her drink, and her pitch long after the Tea Expo ended.

Don't ever let any opportunity to speak pass you by without making the most of it. Remember, no opportunity is too small for you to shine and to be memorable.

• •

SELF-REFLECTION
*When did you take the opportunity to be memorable
and stand out from your competitors?*

• •

52. WHO ARE YOU TRYING TO BE?

In asking a new client about his public speaking challenges, one person kept coming up as a role model: his boss. His boss is authoritative and commanding, while my client feels that he comes off as passive and too easygoing. His boss's voice is strong and powerful, while my client feels that his voice is weak and too soft.

I can't help but wonder to myself: is this true? Is my client really weak and passive and unauthoritative? Is his boss really so wonderful as a presenter?

I will probably never see my client's boss give a presentation, so I can't possibly know how he comes across. But I will see my client give a presentation, and furthermore, I will videotape him so he can see and hear himself. I guarantee that once he sees himself on video, he will begin to develop a more realistic perception of himself as a speaker – and most likely a more positive one, as every other person I've videotaped has done.

The problem lies in our perception of ourselves and in comparing ourselves to others. It's great to have role models to look up to and goals to achieve for improvement, but oftentimes in comparing ourselves to others, we overlook our own strengths and valuable qualities.

Another client is concerned about co-presenting with a colleague who always gets standing ovations. She fears not being able to present at the same level as he does.

We talked about her purpose, her objective, what she wants the audience to do as a result of her presentation. We talked about her passion for the topic and her commitment to getting her message out there. And we talked about giving the audience tools to implement the program she's presenting on.

None of those things have anything to do with getting a standing ovation, so if she gets one, that's great, but she knows that she has more important goals for her presentation than getting the immediate satisfaction of a standing O. Furthermore, she's gotten a lot of positive feedback over the years on her warm, accessible presentation style. She has strengths already; she just has to appreciate them.

Focus on your own strengths and your own challenges as a speaker; comparing yourself to others just leads to disappointment. You can't be someone else. You have your own unique qualities, just as they have theirs. Appreciate your own style, your own voice, and learn how to improve on the you that is already great – in your own way!

• •

SELF-REFLECTION
Who do you compare yourself to and how can you stop?

• •

53. IT TAKES ONLY ONE SENTENCE TO STAND OUT

At one of my monthly networking meetings, each person has an opportunity to introduce themselves in 30 seconds.

Some of the group members don't bother to take advantage of this amazing opportunity to continually improve their pitches. They repeat the same information month after month, never bothering to vary their basic storyline. But I'm happy to say that most of the people in the group do make the effort to engage the rest of us with creative descriptions of what they do and how it benefits their clients and customers.

One of the most effective ways to create a memorable idea that will remain with your audience long after the presentation is to come up with a clever one-liner or sentence that people can connect with. It can be a tagline, a motto, or a slogan, or it can just be a creative way of stating a concept that people will remember. Here are a few I've heard from our group members.

Ellen sells nontoxic household products. In her recent presentation, she described why she believes so strongly in her products like this: "I want to live until I die." She meant that she doesn't want to live a long life but be incapacitated. She wants to be living an active lifestyle till the end. Succinct and powerful.

She also stated, "Good health is an investment, not a purchase." I thought this was such a standout line that I considered stealing it and tweaking it for my business!
Stephanie, an optometrist, gave us this clever and profound reminder to get our eyes checked: "When your world is in focus, you can connect with it better."

And then there was Russell, a painter, whose deadpan delivery was the icing on the cake. This line became an instant classic: "I put all the paint where it's supposed to be and none of it where it shouldn't be." He reminds me of my favorite uncle, who always had a clever expression or wisecrack at hand.

It's not easy to come up with a brilliant and memorable one-liner. But when you've got a good one, that one sentence can be the difference between your audience walking away with only a vague memory of your speech and your audience sharing your message with everyone they know.

• •

SELF-REFLECTION
Do you have a catchy or pithy one-liner that has been successful for you? If not, how could you start developing one?

• •

54. FALLING IN LOVE WITH THE REAL YOU

The movie "Alice Adams" stars Katharine Hepburn as a young woman struggling to fit into a circle that has outpaced her, socially and financially. Her father, content with his low-paying and thankless clerical job, is constantly berated by her social-climbing mother, in an attempt to create a life for Alice that will ensure the security of her future – mostly by finding her an affluent mate.

Alice is portrayed as both a comical and a tragic character, where she is repeatedly snubbed and put down by other girls because of her outdated clothing and lack of social status. She "puts on airs" and pretends to be sophisticated around other people, and she has an optimistic attitude that carries her through some demoralizing situations. But in private she is insecure, sad, and lonely.

My question throughout the whole movie was "Who is Alice Adams?" The person I see fakes her way through every social situation and cries by herself in her bedroom at night, embarrassed to tears by her family, her house, her 2-year-old organdy gown, her hand-picked bouquet, and her social failings. But who is Alice, really? She must have something going for her beyond her determination to fit in, but the movie doesn't let us see any of that.

In trying to win the affections of the wealthy Arthur Russell (played by a very young and handsome Fred MacMurray), she never reveals her true self. How can Arthur fall in love with her if he doesn't know who she really is?

And this leads me to my question for you: **How can your audiences love you if they don't know you?**

As a speaker, how much time and effort are you spending pretending to be something or somebody you're not?

How much time and effort are you putting into cultivating a character who dresses, speaks, and gestures a certain way?

Is that you? Or are you trying to be like someone whose keynote you liked at a conference or someone who won a Toastmasters competition?

Here's what Alice has to say about pretending to be someone she's not, once she's seen the light:

"You do thus and so; and you tell yourself, 'Now, seeing me do thus and so, people will naturally think this and that'; but they don't. They think something else – usually just what you **don't** want 'em to. I suppose about the only good in pretending is the fun we get out of fooling ourselves that we fool somebody." (This is from the book, not the movie.)

She nails it. When you pretend to be someone or something you're not:

🕮 People aren't fooled.

🕮 People are fooled, but not in the way you want them to be.

🕮 People are fooled – and then feel betrayed when they do discover the real you, as they inevitably will.

In the movie, Alice's pretense doesn't stand in the way of her getting her man, even after several humiliating events, including a disastrous dinner meant to impress Arthur on a sweltering summer night. It's Hollywood, after all. (In the book, however, Alice is dumped by Arthur and goes on to business school – apparently a dreaded option leading to spinsterhood. Ah, the 1920s.)

In real life, pretending to be someone you're not leads to more hiding, more deception, and more pressure as you attempt to manipulate and protect the public's perception of you. Being yourself, on the other hand, leads to an incredible sense of liberation. No pretense, no faking it, no mimicking others to try to get the same approval and response.

Pinpoint your unique qualities. Appreciate them. Savor them. Use them. Never be ashamed of who you are or where you are in your life.

Your audience will appreciate (and maybe even love) you for it.

• •

SELF-REFLECTION
How can you fall in love with the real you?
How can your audience?

• •

8 CHANGE YOUR
MINDSET

"People are not afraid of things,
but of how they view them."
— Epictetus —

This is mindset in a nutshell. Your mindset includes all the ideas and attitudes with which you approach a situation. Your mindset includes your beliefs and your thoughts, and regarding speaking, we'll focus on the negative thoughts and limiting beliefs that are keeping you from sharing the message and transformation that your audiences need from you. We'll also talk about how a positive mindset can take you places you never imagined.

It's our interpretation of situations and the meaning we give them that determines our mindset. As Epictetus pointed out so long ago, the reality is going to be the same no matter what we choose to think about it. The reality is that we have no control over the situation, only how we perceive it. Your negative thoughts are there to protect you, but in reality they may be limiting you.

Many of our fears as well as our negative thoughts and beliefs about public speaking (and other things) are only vaguely based in reality, if at all. I will quote myself here: "If our mind is powerful enough to create fear from 'nothing,' it's also powerful enough to reframe our thoughts to propel us forward in a positive way."

Here's one way to think about speaking mindset.

Have you ever been on a date?

Did you enjoy it? Did you hate it? You've probably had both experiences!

Did you ask the other person out? Did they ask you out? Maybe you've just kind of eased into it by saying "We should do something sometime." (I used that one on my hubby when we were still getting to know each other.)

Did/do you find dating stressful? Scary? Uncomfortable? Nervewracking?

Did/do you feel like you were on display? Being judged?

There is an important purpose behind dating: You hope to find your soulmate, your life partner, or at least someone you enjoy being with for a while. Most of us would like to have a special someone in our lives that we can share some level of intimacy with, and dating helps us find that person.

Dating also helps you discover who you are as a person. Dating helps you test out who you are and who you want to be in a relationship. Dating helps you work on your communication skills, your self-awareness, your self-perceptions and what kind of person you are on the inside.

As much as dating can feel awkward and uncomfortable, you do it because there's a desired outcome and reward. You may feel nervous about it, but you still do it, because you understand the value behind it.

Public speaking also has desired outcomes and rewards. There is incredible value to getting in front of an audience and sharing your message.

Avoiding public speaking because it's scary and you have to face the unknown is like avoiding dating because it's scary and you have to face the unknown.

What if you were to perceive the rewards of speaking the way you perceive the rewards of dating?

What if your biggest dreams of personal and professional success could be met just by getting in front of more audiences and giving more memorable and engaging presentations?

Mindset is key to taking risks and putting yourself out there in front of audiences – even though it might be scary!

In this section, look for lessons for speakers using examples from my childhood babysitter, a world champion figure skater, and the drought in California.

55. BIG BROWN EYES

When I was young, before I started school, I would go to the home of a childcare provider during the week while my parents worked.

One day, this babysitter told my friend Debbie that she had beautiful big brown eyes. I was standing next to Debbie, so I asked, "Do I have big brown eyes?" The babysitter said, "No, you have little eyes."

I must have been four years old, and to this day, I still remember this discouraging comment.

I don't worry about my freakishly small eyes anymore; I figured out at some point that they're normal – no better or worse than anyone else's eyes.

But it still shocks me how one thoughtless comment (even a misinterpreted one) can stay with us literally forever – like the comment from my theater professor who thought I should get out of acting because of my lisp.
I don't dwell on that anymore, either. It's a part of who I am. Period.

We all have our insecurities. Some of those insecurities have nothing to do with reality and are based on some fantasy we've concocted in our heads. Some have more to do with some mean comment someone made 15 years ago, or the influence of the media, our culture, or community.

Some of us let those insecurities hold us back and keep us from achieving the things we want to achieve.

When I was in high school, I worried a lot about how people perceived me, like most of us going through those years of self-discovery. I regularly made New Year's resolutions in my journal to "stop being so loud," "stop being a spaz," "try to be more calm," and "mellow out." Sometimes I felt like a real clown.

But at the same time I was also journaling, "Don't let individuality get me down." "Be myself." Yes, these are directly from my diary.

Then I became a theater major, and suddenly all those aspects of my personality that I had tried to squash made sense. They fit. I realized, "This is who I am!"

Once I found a way to embrace my quirky qualities, I was a much happier person.

Are you able to move past those remarks and negative influences, hold your head high, embrace who you are, and do what you want to do – regardless of what others might think?

• •

SELF-REFLECTION
What ancient insecurities are you allowing to hold you back?

• •

56. IN SPEAKING, AS IN SPORTS, THE REWARD OUTWEIGHS THE RISK

The Winter Olympics are full of risk-taking athletes. They jump, they spin, they twirl, they flip, they slide, they glide, and they push as hard as they can – all at the risk of falling on their behinds and losing time, points, and medals.

The athletes know they might fall down, and even face serious injury, but that doesn't keep them from performing at the highest level.

Two-time world champion figure skater Mao Asada, one of a handful of skaters who has landed a triple axel in competition, was the hot topic of conversation a few years ago. Would she be able to accomplish this high-scoring feat during her short program?

Asada attempted but did not land her axel in the ladies' short program. She was a favorite for the gold medal and was the reigning silver medalist. She took the risk and didn't succeed, in fact, falling down to 16th place.

But the potential reward was worth it for her. She still performed her long program like a champion and – guess what – she landed the triple axel and a variety of other triples and combinations. Unfortunately, she was out of the running for a medal, finishing in sixth place. In the end, her score was a personal record.

Was she disappointed not to win a medal? Of course. Do you think she regrets taking the risk? Not for a minute. She said to a reporter, "With this performance, I could thank all the people who supported me all this time."

There are snowboarders and skiers who try extremely risky tricks, some of which they've only completed in practice and never in competition. But the potential reward outweighs the risk, which is why they do it. The chance of representing your country with a gold medal is a huge motivation, not to mention delivering personal best performances and justifying years of hard work.

How does the reward of speaking outweigh the risk for you?

We all experience some risk when we get in front of an audience. We know there's a chance we might come across as less than stellar, that the performance we imagine in our heads might be a whole different thing in reality. We know we might forget our words, have a technology breakdown, or demonstrate our nervousness with shaking hands or quivering voice.

But are these risks really so huge when you think about the rewards?

Some of the rewards of speaking include:

- You get the opportunity to share your message with a captive audience.

- You get to stand out from all those people who avoid speaking.

- You get to learn about yourself as a person and face your personal challenges.

- You get to connect with people and build relationships.

- You get to work on your skills every time you're on the stage or in the conference room.

- You get to help people move forward and take action.

- You get to express your ideas, change minds, and make an impact.

- You get to be in charge of the room – and own the stage.

There is so much a speaker gets out of presenting to an audience. You get to be your most fabulous, bold, brilliant, witty self. You get to stand out while others hide in the shadows. You get to change minds, and maybe lives.

You're not in danger when you speak. You're not going to get a concussion or tear your ACL. You're not going to be fired or shunned from society. The rewards far outweigh the risks. So what are you waiting for?

• •

SELF-REFLECTION
What risks are you willing to take to up your game?

• •

57. GET ALL THE RESULTS WITH NONE OF THE EFFORT

Just kidding. You know that's not how it works, right?

I would like to lose twenty pounds. In fact, I would like my body to look the way it did in my 30s. But here's the problem: I'm older, it's harder, and I'm not making the commitment to do the work. Back then I was at the gym six days a week, lifting heavy weights and doing cardio. Six days a week.

I eat pretty well, as a vegetarian, but also love sweets and wine too much (well, that's what my triglycerides are telling me). If I really want my body to be the way it was at my peak of fitness, I need to do the work.

I read magazine articles and books about healthy eating and exercise. And I'm an expert on what works for my own body. I know exactly what I could be doing to get back into shape. But I don't make the effort. I don't discipline myself. I don't make the right choices. So I stay the way I am.

I know you hope your presentations will magically improve without the work. I know you hope that, by reading articles and books and watching TED speakers, you'll become a more effective and engaging speaker by osmosis. I know you know you could be doing better.

But better requires work. There's just no way around it.

It requires learning what makes a presentation effective, and then using and practicing those tools and techniques.

It requires preparing way more than you're preparing now.

It requires changing your attitude about public speaking and about how you serve your audience.

It requires getting feedback from legitimate sources, not from people who are afraid to hurt your feelings or want to keep their job.

And it requires accepting most speaking engagements that comes your way – most of the time – and making opportunities when they're not coming your way.

But you don't want to do the work. I hear you. Believe me, I get it.

I don't want to be a big bummer. The internet is full of people who tell you how to "lose ten pounds in a week" and "make millions of dollars while you sleep." I'm not one of those people. Losing ten pounds in a week is a temporary condition caused by diuretics. Making money while you sleep? Yep, that still takes a lot of work. While you're awake.

Your presentations won't change if you don't make the effort. Your PowerPoint will still be riddled with tiny text and too many bullets. Your content will be disorganized or boring, or just mediocre. Your delivery will be disconnected or mechanical, or just unmemorable.

And my body is going to stay the same: flabby, with this extra twenty pounds, unless we stop fantasizing and start **doing**.

So here's what I propose: You and I, let's take baby steps.

Here's what I'm doing: I've cut back on snacking during the day, and especially at night, which is when I'm the least disciplined. I'm portioning out my snacks so that I eat one serving, not one bag! And I'm sticking with my doctor's suggestion of no more than seven glasses of wine in a week. Not so hard.

What's one thing can you do – one baby step – to start making your presentations better?

We can do it, you and I.

● ●

SELF-REFLECTION
What choices will get your presentations to the next level?

● ●

58. IS YOUR MENTAL GAME UP TO PAR?

I recently watched a documentary about a group of cyclists who race 2,700+ miles from the Canadian border to the Mexican border along the Continental Divide. The race is called the Tour Divide, an "ultra-cycling challenge to pedal solo and self-supported the length of Great Divide Mountain Bike Route ... as fast as possible."

Only a few people attempt it and fewer finish (in 2010, the last year I can find data for, 48 started and 23 finished). One competitor who had a particularly hard time was Mary Metcalf-Collier, who suffered physical hardships along the way, including severe swelling in her legs.

She came close to quitting many times, but she knew the key to staying in the race was her "mental game," and she continued to push herself past her discomfort, eventually becoming the first woman to complete the race.

She says in her blog, "The most important lesson that I picked up last year was about flexibility. As I read back through my journals from 2008, I probably had 3 days total that went exactly as planned."

Most of us aren't facing this level of physical pain when preparing for a presentation. But many speakers' mental game is not up to the challenge of overcoming anxiety and the resulting resistance and avoidance.

The mental game of speaking includes:

1. Planning and preparation for things that might go wrong

What happens if your computer crashes in the middle of your PowerPoint? What happens if you lose your place? What happens if someone gives you a hard time during Q&A? Are you prepared?

2. Reframing anxiety and nervousness into positive attitude and energy

There is no difference between "bad" and "good" adrenaline – it's your mind that makes it so. Thought stopping, positive self-talk, relaxation, and other mental and physical tools can get you in a calmer state to face your audience.

3. Visualizing a successful presentation

Have you visited the venue in advance so you know the layout of the room and any challenges? Have you envisioned yourself in front of a satisfied and smiling audience, giving waves of applause? Successful elite athletes use visualization and mental rehearsal both to imagine a successful outcome of an event and to rest and relax.

4. Giving 100% when you only feel 50%

Got the flu, but can't find a replacement? Performing on two hours of sleep?

Distracted by personal problems? Your audience can't and shouldn't know this. Give them what they came for and rest later.

5. Handling mishaps onstage in the moment with grace and humor

Everyone makes mistakes and most of the time your audience doesn't even know you've messed up. Suck it up, laugh it off, and move on!

6. Being flexible

Sometimes you're prepared to speak for an hour, but the speaker or meeting before you goes long and your time gets cut. Sometimes you expect an audience of fifty, and it ends up being an audience of five. Sometimes you get stuck with a microphone that's attached to a lectern and you're frozen in place. Having a strong mental game means being able to shift gears at a moment's notice, take what you're given, and run with it.

• •

SELF-REFLECTION
How can you strengthen your mental game as a speaker?

• •

59. WANT TO IMPROVE AS A SPEAKER? CHANGE YOUR ATTITUDE!

I came across the following status update on Facebook one morning from an old friend who's just moved to another state and started a new job:

"Not sure what I think about getting ready for work at 4:30 am."

My first thought – of course – was UGH. I'm not a morning person. It's torture for me to get out of bed before 8:30 most days.

But the very first comment to her post was this: "You think it's awesome!"

And further down the page: "That you are so happy to have a great job!! :) Drink lots of coffee!!"

And I just got all warm and fuzzy inside. **It's really about attitude, isn't it?**

I spoke to a client yesterday who told me he sits in company meetings thinking to himself, "Don't ask me to speak. Don't ask me to speak."

I suggested to him that, instead of sitting in meetings hoping not to get called on, instead he should attend meetings with the **intention** to speak. If he plans something to say – give a report, tell a joke, make an announcement – then the fear of being called on has no validity. He's calling on himself!

So now, instead of dreading being asked to speak, he's making the decision to speak and taking control of the situation.

So much anxiety about public speaking comes from giving negative mental energy to the wrong things, the things we fear we can't control. Well, the truth is, we can't control everything. So how about we control what we can and let the rest fall into place? Wanna know what you can always control? Your attitude!

Instead of "I hate public speaking," how about "If I got more practice, I might become better at public speaking and enjoy it more."

Instead of "I'm going to make a mistake and embarrass myself," how about, "I might make a mistake, but so what? I'm human. I can laugh it off and move on."

Instead of "I'm going to bore the audience," how about, "I have valuable things to say and I'm excited to share!"

Instead of "I can't believe I have to give this stupid report," how about, "I'm so lucky to have the opportunity to practice my speaking skills and show my department how confident and self-assured I am. I deserve the promotion that's coming to me!"

Change your attitude and you change everything, most importantly your ability to learn, improve, and grow.

. . . .

SELF-REFLECTION
*What steps can you take to create
a more positive attitude for yourself?*

. . . .

60. WHAT SELF-DOUBTS ARE KEEPING YOU FROM THE STAGE?

I wrote earlier about hanging onto insecurities for way too long, like when my babysitter told me that I had "little eyes" and I hung onto that horrible perceived flaw for decades.

I spoke to two people recently who have been holding onto perceived defects for many years without getting any feedback to change their views. These "defects" have led to great insecurity over time, but fortunately, they called me! And I set them straight.

The first client told me she was self-conscious about her accent. She grew up speaking multiple languages and didn't move to the United States until her teens. It's one of the main things holding her back from getting out there in front of audiences. But guess what: **She doesn't even have an accent!**

At least, her accent is so minor and so insignificant that it will be unnoticeable to 99% of people who hear her speak. And to that remaining 1%, they might think she's a typical southern California native who grew up speaking English, but maybe had parents from another country.

I never would have guessed that she grew up speaking three Asian languages in addition to English, and I never would have guessed that she wasn't born here. Her accent is minimal, her grasp of English is perfect, and this is absolutely a non-issue.

When I told her this, the relief she expressed was phenomenal. She's never gotten feedback on her voice and had built up this terrible lack of confidence and self-consciousness about her accent. I realize her self-consciousness won't go away overnight, but this is the first time anyone has told her that her accent is negligible.

I also spoke to a man this week who thinks he has a terrible speaking voice because – 40 years ago – a vocal coach in college told him he did.

Wow. Can you imagine (I bet you can ...) carrying around something like this for 40 years? Thinking you have a terrible voice because one person so long ago gave you this feedback?

Again, I set him straight. He doesn't have a terrible speaking voice in any way, shape, or form. Yes, he can probably improve his speaking voice, like most of us can if we're going to spend a lot of time on stage. But "can improve" is a long way from "terrible."

Are you carrying around some deep-seated insecurity about your voice, your appearance, your abilities, your mannerisms, or something else that's holding you back from the stage? And if so, have you actually gotten feedback on this perceived imperfection, or are you perhaps blowing it out of proportion because someone told you a long time ago that this was something "wrong" with you and it's gotten bigger and uglier over time?

Get feedback from a neutral party. Find out if it's all in your head. Because in order to move forward you have to determine if this is something that's even a problem. If it is, then by all means make the effort to fix it. But if it's not, wouldn't you rather just let it go?

• •

SELF-REFLECTION
What self-doubts are all in your head?
How can you identify them and let them go?

• •

61. OPTIMISM: FINDING THE UPSIDE OF THE INEVITABLE

As I write this section, California has come to the end of several rainy seasons with below-seasonal totals. The ongoing severe drought is our #1 concern here, and every day that goes by without rain puts us more and more into a water deficit.

A cousin commented on one of my Facebook posts: "So much for the El Niño predictions last summer and fall. Can't believe how wrong they were."

My immediate response: "Maybe it's good to have hope instead of feeling completely hopeless!"

Welcome to the mind of an optimist. A perpetual silver-lining finder. A person for whom the song "High Hopes" is my true life story. (My #2 strength in the StrengthsFinder assessment is Positivity. Go figure.)

At the time of that Facebook comment, I'd been sick for almost a week, and not a mild sniffle, but a raging, persistent, mean, and nasty cold. And I had a flight to catch out of state in two days. How does an optimist look at a problem like this?

Here's how the process went in my brain:

"Well, at least I didn't get as sick as my husband, who had a fever and had to go to urgent care after three days of razor blades in his throat."

"It's a good thing my hotel roommate in Austin didn't book our room for Thursday, because there's no way I could fly out on Thursday. I'll probably feel better by Friday."

"If I fly to Austin on Friday, I can check into my hotel and rest all day. I can hold off on going to conference sessions until Saturday."

Sadly, I did have to cancel my trip to the conference in Austin. No amount of optimism could fight that virus in time!

But see how it works? Yes, it comes naturally to me. It's just the way I'm wired. But you can **learn** optimism.

And why should a speaker learn optimism?

Imagine you're invited to speak at an event that you're very nervous about. You can choose your perception about this event. You can choose your attitude about this event.

You can tell yourself one of two things:

> *"I'm going to make a mistake, and the whole thing is going to be a disaster."*

> *. . . OR . . .*

> *"I'm going to make a mistake, but I'm human and everyone makes mistakes. No big deal."*

Notice how both of these predictions have a sense of reality? Yes, optimists face reality. As a speaker, you absolutely have to be prepared for mistakes and mishaps. It would just be foolish to believe that nothing will go wrong.

But then we figure out how we can find the upside of the inevitable.

Wouldn't this be a better approach as a speaker? To look at your speaking engagements as opportunities to accomplish something – even small somethings – rather than expecting certain failure?

And by the way, before I ever heard of Martin Seligman's concept of "Learned Optimism," I knew this was true. Despite my genetic disposition toward optimism, I've been through some very difficult times where my positive outlook took a nosedive. My willingness to keep looking for the light at the end of the tunnel and my willingness to believe that everything is a learning experience got me through those times. And sometimes I had to force myself to really dig for those silver linings.

Seligman's website says, "Specifically, optimistic people believe that negative events are temporary, limited in scope (instead of pervading every aspect of a person's life), and manageable….People can also change their levels of optimism depending on the situations they are in."

A client told me about an experience where he had to record a radio commercial. It could have been nerve-wracking for him, but he felt surprisingly confident about it because he chose his attitude: "There was no reason to believe it wouldn't go well." He told himself that he was in control of his own response to the situation.

This particular client has **a lot** of anxiety about speaking. It's not easy for him to make this mental shift. Not even close. But he is learning optimism. He is learning to become more philosophical about how he perceives his speaking opportunities. Instead of choosing "Every reason to believe it will go wrong," he chooses "No reason to believe it won't go well."

So I didn't get to go to the conference, and that was a bummer. But here's the new silver lining: Because I caught the virus early enough, I was completely recovered by the time my 2½-day retreat a few weeks later was scheduled to begin.

●●●

SELF-REFLECTION
You can do this. You can change your thoughts.
How can you choose optimism?

●●●

FINAL THOUGHTS

Before I wrap up, I want to share some of the ideas that have come my way over the years for making your presentations more fun. Enjoy the silliness and see if any of these examples stimulate your funny bone.

"A member of the Board of Realtors started the meeting by asking questions and throwing candy to people who got the answer right. He didn't say he was going to; he just did for the first right answer. Then, of course, we all wanted to answer his questions! He started this way to get an idea where his audience was on the topic. It really got us interested in an otherwise boring subject!"

"Start out with this: 'TAP TAP TAP, is this thing on? Can you hear me? I'd like to propose a toast to the bride and groom, but seriously folks…' Gets a laugh every time…"

"I love this getting-to-know-you activity: Each person brings out their keys and takes a minute to tell about their keys, what they go to, where the keychain came from and why they chose it."

"At a corporate social responsibility forum at a posh hotel in Shanghai, a speaker came up to the microphone and silently touched up her makeup…. She then explained that many companies approach corporate social responsibility as makeup to cover blemishes, before transitioning into her discussion of the foundational role that it should play in any business.

Totally unexpected and thought-provoking...."

"I once gave a presentation on 'Sexual Harassment and Disparaging terms' in the military. I used the 'Sexual Harassment Panda' scene from South Park and then used a SNL skit where 'Sean Connery' calls 'Alex Trebec's' mother a whore. Both got laughs from my audience and helped break the ice."

"I tend to build different fun items into each presentation. My favorite was in a presentation on how to build ideas that 'stick' in the mind. Each participant had a couple of plastic golf balls. Half of them had Velcro strips attached, while the other half did not. At the appropriate time I put on a ridiculous knit cap and had them all throw their balls at me. Just enough stuck to make my point."

"At each lunch table during a conference – ask each table to come up with a humorous riddle based on the conference content. The table spokesperson shares with the room."

"I do one of several magic tricks to illustrate what I'm presenting or teaching, e.g., needle through balloon, always-full water pitcher that I empty out several times, etc."

"I enjoy giving out door prizes at the end. It works a lot better than it sounds – very much **not** game show, though I do add some 'you could win' excitement. They're all relevant to the productivity topic: three Super Spy Night Pens, and a labeler (grand prize). I've actually seen some NASA clients almost get into a fight over the pens."

(LB: This is one of mine) I founded a nonprofit organization back in 1997, and each year we held an orientation for new volunteers. Part of the training involved a journey through the history of the organization. We unrolled a long piece of butcher paper with the timeline of the organization drawn on it. Each volunteer had pulled a participation card with a number on it, and at strategic points during the presentation, the butcher paper drawing would unroll further to show a number that corresponded to the volunteer's card.

The volunteer would read what was on the card – sometimes something funny and sometimes a point of history. There were also big asterisks placed throughout the drawing to represent milestones, and when we would come to those spots on the drawing, everyone in the room would make a bunch of noise with noisemakers. It was a fun way to explore a subject that might otherwise be considered boring, but was necessary for our volunteers to understand.

And one more from the volunteer orientation…

The mission of the nonprofit I co-founded was to promote the participation, recognition, and celebration of local women and girls in sports and physical activity. As a gender-equity organization, we had a lot to teach our volunteers about not just the history of gender equity and Title IX, but also about the pioneers of women's sports who had paved the way for all of us.

I created a Pioneer Women bingo game that had women's names laid out in a grid of 25 squares. We played as you usually play bingo, calling out names in each square, but each time a name was called, we had someone in the room give a brief bio and accomplishments of the woman whose name was called. It was an engaging way of learning about women's sports pioneers. We also played this game laid out on the floor with pieces of paper creating the bingo "card."

My philosophy of speaking is that it's fun, that it's an awesome way to express yourself creatively, and that connection and engagement are worth more than a thousand techniques.

As you've noticed from reading this book, I don't approach speaking in the traditional way, with a lot of rules or rigid instruction. I'm always coming from a place of building relationships with my audiences. My core belief that informs everything I do is "**Being real creates connection.**"

I hope that I've been able to convey my love of public speaking through this book. I hope it inspires you to have more fun on stage, take yourself less seriously, and make that human connection that your audiences crave. And I hope it inspires you to find new speaking lessons for yourself through your everyday encounters and experiences.

Visit my website to find downloads, worksheets and checklists that accompany this book: www.coachlisab.com/pfh-form.html.

ABOUT THE
AUTHOR

Through individual coaching, corporate training, virtual group programs and live retreats, **Lisa Braithwaite** mentors entrepreneurs and professionals to deliver memorable and engaging presentations in order to build their businesses through speaking.

Lisa is also a food hobbyist, a tea enthusiast, a vegetarian, a cat lover, a bird watcher, a jewelry maker, an Anglophile, a word nerd, and a fan of crime shows and espionage movies—all potential inspiration for her writing.

She lives in Ojai, California with her husband and kitty.

Find more information on Lisa's offerings at coachlisab.com.

CPSIA information can be obtained
at www.ICGtesting.com
Printed in the USA
LVHW09s2122041018
592388LV00001B/192/P

9 780998 171418